PHOENIX RISING

*A Mother's Journey
Through Life and Loss*

Judy Giovangelo

Copyright ©2018 Judy Giovangelo

ISBN-13:9781719228626
ISBN-10:1719228620

Published by Dream Factory Press
Design and Editing by Ellen Keiter, Ellen's Arts
Set in Palatino

10. 9 8 7 6 5 4 3 2

Library of Congress Cataloging in Publication Data
Giovangelo, Judy
Phoenix Rising: A Mother's Journey Through Life and Loss

Life
> *Phoenix Rising: A Mother's Journey Through Life and Loss by Judy Giovangelo*

Death
> *Phoenix Rising: A Mother's Journey Through Life and Loss by Judy Giovangelo*

Suicide
> *Phoenix Rising: A Mother's Journey Through Life and Loss by Judy Giovangelo*

For my son Benjamin and all the Bens still out there,
for anyone raising, teaching or concerned about a Ben—
a struggling youth in your community—
and
for any parent who has lost a Ben

My Three Bens

Who is a Ben?
A Ben beats to his own drum from the moment he is born.
A Ben is creative, artistic, sensitive and empathic.
A Ben does not fit the mainstream model for learning.
A Ben draws outside the lines.
A Ben is rebellious and can be extremely challenging.
A Ben is bullied and often becomes one himself.
A Ben is labelled early and usually medicated.
A Ben isolates socially in his teens.
A Ben tends to self-medicate and engages in self-harm.
A Ben is not broken.
A Ben has gifts to bring to this world!
And . . . there's a little bit of Ben in all of us!

You never really know . . . unless you've lived it . . .

The daily challenge of raising a mentally ill child who looks normal, but isn't.

*Never knowing when, how, where or **why** this disease will rear its ugly head.*

Not being able to control it, fix it or change it . . . when it does appear.

The desperate search for resources and support from community that came in small doses.

The sometimes subtle and more often blatant blind eye, turned shoulder, judgment or criticism from others.

Living in a fishbowl, where the whole world gets to see your pain and judges you rather than supports you.

The whispers behind your back that you can feel from others whose children are normal. (Lucky them!)

The comments from family and friends who think they could do better. (I hope they never have to.)

Watching rocks being thrown at your child by a bully while the bystander laughs.

Watching that child try so hard to fit in.

Watching that child be shunned . . . over and over and over again.

The impossible task of buffering your other two children from the daily consequences of mental illness.

The constant search for compassion, understanding, tolerance and acceptance.

The deep-seated fear of losing your child.

Witnessing your daughter find her brother dead by his own hand.

The devastation and judgment of suicide.

The freedom of suicide.

The guilt from the freedom of suicide.

The collateral damage of suicide.

The pain in your heart that you must bear until your own dying day.

The burden of grief from eighteen years of unfair treatment.

The self-doubt that comes from that internal voice that says what all the outside voices confirm: "It's your fault."

> *Oh, the voice, the voice we must all face.*
> *Oh the choice, the choice we must all embrace.*

Today, I choose love.

Ben and Me

TABLE OF CONTENTS

HOW THIS STORY CAME TO BE

I have often wondered if this story would ever be told. Benjamin and I had a plan to someday share our profound and out-of-the-box story of healing miracles, to provide inspiration, hope and insight to others plagued with similar challenges and lessons.

Sadly, this story emerges now from devastating circumstances: we lost our son Benjamin to suicide after eighteen years of our family suffering with the stigma of mental illness. Ben himself was continuously bullied and ostracized by his peers—and his community at large. He ended his life in a fleeting moment of despair, when his pain became greater than the resources available to him in that moment.

I cannot even begin to know what it was like to be inside Ben's skin, but I have a first-hand account and eighteen years of my own experience as his mom as testimony. It is my intention to share my experience with you: to awaken the power of choice we all have in order to navigate the inherent challenges in life, and to be the change regardless of what we face. It is my personal mission, through this book of essays, to share the extraordinary spiritual journey of my continued relationship with my son's spirit as the catalyst for my work and the profound messages of hope I have received along the way.

Gratefully, I have learned to trust the voice of Spirit above all else. I have learned to listen to my heart more than my head, and to cultivate my own innate gifts. Most importantly, I have learned to remember always that *I matter* and that my contribution to this planet counts. You see . . . *I am also a Ben.*

1

JUDY'S STORY

It's not a decision to be different. Each of us is born to be something glorious, magnificent—to beat to our own drum, to our own pulse. At the same time, we are born with an innate desire to belong. From the moment I arrived into the world it was clear I was different. A misfit of sorts. I remember as a child at Christmastime watching Rudolph, the Red-Nosed Reindeer, every time the broken toys were sent to the Island of Misfit Toys I would weep. I could relate so profoundly.

In my home in upstate New York I was bullied and picked on by my siblings. My older sisters compared me to my baby sister Sue: they loved her and rejected me. I could feel it, hear it, and see it in their actions. At three years old this belief or early imprint was set in stone in my mind when my oldest brother Stephen wrote a song called "Sue Sue, the Greatest Sue Sue." He would play it on his guitar with the whole family singing it to her as she bounced lovingly on Daddy's knee. Daddy's knee was never a place I had been invited to. This drove the early belief of being a misfit deep into the blueprint of my subconscious mind.

When I went to school at age five, I began a lifetime of not fitting in. I didn't know why and—God help me—I tried for most of my life. Everywhere I went, whether at school or at home, I felt judged, wronged and left out, and had a sinking feeling that just being me was not good enough.

My happiest times as a child were when I was alone in the woods behind my house creating a world of characters that loved me and accepted me. I played by myself in the trees and the soft pine forest . . . until I was nine years old and was yanked from my childhood fantasy: my father decided to move us from upstate New York to Florida. Like Dorothy in *The Wizard of Oz*, I was literally transported from the safety of my childhood environment to being a stranger in a strange land. I was completely out of my element and felt unprotected as my family shattered upon arriving in the Sunshine State. Within only months of our upheaval, my father asked my mother for a divorce, and left her penniless and alone with four of her six children.

Lynn, the oldest of the clan, had been abandoned at twenty years old in college back in upstate New York, witnessing her family fall apart far, far away from what was home her whole life. My brother Steve was a nomad who left home at eighteen to forge his own life, and didn't think twice about thumbing across the country.

In our new home in Florida, my sister Candace became my mother figure as my mom was forced back to work to feed her family. She had been ripped from her first love and her high school family at the tumultuous age of sixteen, and consequently took out the frustrations of her dismantled life on me. I was the middle child of the three youngest: Mark, Judy and Sue. Mark and Sue were the babies—Mark being the youngest boy—and both were adorable. I was the "ugly duckling" and for many years felt left out and picked on by all three of my siblings. Candace would actually go out of her way to tease me, berate me, pit my siblings against me, creating drama that left me feeling powerless and unloved. In later years, she told me she took her pain out on me because she didn't feel good about herself, and I eventually forgave her.

Between the ages of twelve and fifteen, my brother Mark and his friends—who gathered daily at my dining room table to play drinking games and get plastered while my mom was working—would verbally and sometimes physically abuse me. My full name was Judith Newcomb Hopkins, so they would call me "Nukie" or "Rude Rudy" and would laugh at me and taunt me right there in my own home. On many occasions they would push me, shove me, or pass me around like a Tinkertoy as they added insult to injury. Believe me, I was no angel, and I am sure each of my siblings has a very different perspective of our upbringing. This is my story.

Over the years, I became reactive and rebellious and turned into what my mother would call an "itch" or "a pain in the ass." Understandably so. The biggest kick to my already diminished self-worth happened when my mom took the family to therapy. I believe I was around thirteen. At this point, we were all drinking, smoking weed and cigarettes and skipping out of school when my mother went to work. I remember the therapist inviting us to play-act a scene: he wanted everyone to focus on where they thought the root of the problem in the home was. They all looked at me. I was, in that moment, wounded to my core. I never experienced such betrayal in all my life. I refused to go back. I don't think I ever did, although those years are a blur to me now.

It has taken me decades of therapy and healing work to undo the deep-seated belief that everything is my fault. I developed a defensiveness in my younger years that to this day is still a challenge for me. I know now that we are all products of our environment, and that our ego and our need to be right and survive is what motivates the behaviors that both my siblings and I displayed back then. Ultimately, I have chosen to forgive and replace the deeply planted seeds of insecurity, blame and not being enough with a deeper knowing that all of my experiences have been opportunities to find my way back to love—first for myself and, over time, for all of those around me.

And then—during this time of complete insanity for this pre-teen abused mess—there were the events I was completely powerless to control. Ok, I didn't have the "lions and tigers and bears, oh my!" like Dorothy in *The Wizard of Oz*. I wish it had been that easy. For me it was "tornados and hurricanes and fires, oh my!" Add to that: severe flooding, disastrous and frightening trips to sea with my drunken father, warding off a next-door-neighbor sex offender, and almost losing our home to a fire set by my mother's drunken boyfriend. The Lollipop Kids were the teenage drug dealers who were my brother Mark's friends—and, on top of that, the Good Witch in *this* story did not exist. Bad witches were a-plenty and the forest of my life was filled with chaos and multiple near-death experiences.

During those years, lacking in resources and support, I went into a very dark hole. I seriously wanted to die and found myself dousing my little body and mind with every drug known to man, short of heroin. I cut my arms in hopes of bleeding to death and prayed for God to take me.

Finally and eventually, it became acutely clear to me that I had a different way of learning things. I had no capability of expressing what I was feeling, and in those days there were no markers or language for learning differences. It wasn't until my own son Ben was tested in high school that I realized that *I* struggled with similar brain deficiencies—or what I call today "brain design challenges." I am not a linear thinker and when information is coming at me, it gets scrambled. I have to find my own process of putting the pieces into a pattern that makes sense to me.

For most of my life teachers have embarrassed me, making me feel stupid for not being able to understand or grasp certain concepts. They would become frustrated because they couldn't help me understand. As you can imagine, this reinforced the belief there was something fundamentally wrong with me. At sixteen, as soon as it was legally my decision, I dropped out of high school.

Yes, I am the kid from the school of hard knocks. However, I made a decision to pull my life out of that deep hole. At seventeen I went back to school and got my GED (the equivalent of a high school diploma)—which I passed with flying colors. Yup . . . pretty darn smart. I graduated at eighteen and a half with a secretarial degree, left the state of Florida with my oldest sister Lynn (who I barely knew), and never looked back.

This began my journey out of the downward spiral and toward a better life. Leaving Florida was the best decision I ever made, and was the first of many new choices that shifted my life in a huge way.

Now barely nineteen and settled in Boston with my aunt and uncle in Hyde Park, I spent several years moving from job to job around the city, honing my skills as a secretary and administrative assistant. I had always had an interest in the physical body and now had a burning desire to go back to school or get trained in some part of the medical field. Because of the lack of finances available to me, I considered joining the Navy to become an X-ray technician and even took the test for it.

It was during that time, while working as secretary for the president of the Boston Molasses Company in South Boston, that I met Tom, my future husband. I fell in love with him from the moment I saw him, and let go of my dream of joining the Navy and traveling the world. Six years later, after living together for several of those years, we were married.

I was excited to begin my new chapter as wife and mother. I had always wanted children. I wanted more than anything to give my children what I had always desired for myself: to be loved, adored, accepted and cherished for just being me. I am not sure any of us would make the decision to have children if we knew how hard it was going to be. I have no regrets, but it hasn't been easy by any stretch of the imagination. At the same time, parenting has provided me with profound insight and incredible opportunities to learn and grow. It is through my children—especially my middle child Benjamin—that I was able to see myself, heal the wounds of my past, and develop tools to become the calm in the storm of my own life. Somewhere along the way I learned that my greatest power came from within, and that in order to thrive in life I needed to forgive myself, love myself first, and just *grow me*.

2

BENJAMIN

Within months of his birth, I began seeing glimpses of what would later become a grim realization that my beautiful boy, Benjamin, was dealing with something unusual—something that would forever rule his life until his dying day.

Benjamin Joseph Giovangelo was born with every part in place. He appeared to be a seemingly healthy, thriving and bouncing baby boy. He was born on April 10, 1991—two years and nine months after his brother Michael. His easier delivery into the world would mask his later difficulties. The arrival of his sister Jenna two years later would be to his dismay.

At around three months old Ben started to exhibit unusual, unexplainable behavior. Whenever I was within an arm's length of him, he would place his tiny baby hand directly on my throat. Being a young mother, this was truly disconcerting. Every time I would pull his little hand away from my neck, it would be back there within seconds, as though driven by a compulsivity that he couldn't control. It seemed almost automatic.

He was an extremely difficult and obstinate toddler, and rarely went with the flow. His daily episodes of control dramas lasted much longer than what I experienced with his older brother. Michael's terrible twos were a dim memory and nothing out of the norm. With Ben, however, the terrible twos continued into threes, fours and fives.

By the time he was ready for pre-school, Ben had begun to perform what would be lifelong daily rituals that consumed his energy. The challenge of just getting him to school every day went on for years and years. By first grade, he felt he needed to perform ten rituals before he would even enter the school. Unless he did them perfectly the first time, he would have to start over until he got them just right. Later he developed more debilitating rituals, including spitting profusely on his shirt, touching his private parts inappropriately in school, searching for his spirit around every corner, and asking if he was going to get poisoned and die every time he put food to his mouth. The list went on and on.

As though that was not enough for this poor child to deal with, he was also dominated by an incessant need to be in control of everything and everyone within his personal space. He had an uncontrollable desire to claim space, things, people and circumstances—at the cost of dueling to his own death if necessary to achieve domination. Benjamin would be practically willing to die to get his own way. It was as though the voice of reason was an ingredient left out of his gene pool at his creation.

There were days when our daily routine was consumed not only by Ben's rituals, but also by his inability to let go of whatever he wanted in that moment. We would have pockets of reprieve when all was going according to his plan, but as soon as he was told "no," he would become a raging, insane child. These episodes could go on for hours and often happened more than once in a day. They were completely exhausting, and no matter what his father and I did, we couldn't reach him.

Once Ben made it through the doors at school, his behavior was fine. His earlier teachers would report ritualistic behavior, but said it was nothing out of the ordinary. How was it possible that we were experiencing an endless stream of unreasonableness at home, yet in school he was a delightful, go-with-the-flow kind of child? This made no sense and went right to the part of me that felt somehow responsible. If Ben was misbehaving only with me, then *I* must be doing something wrong.

I could recall countless episodes from the past, but there are a few doozies that I will share here to paint the picture for you. There was nothing like being in a public place when Ben went into a tirade. I will never forget one of our trips to Florida, and more importantly, for this part of the story, our visit to Sea World. Ben was in rare form that day. He was only three years old. The day started off great. It was a beautiful morning and it felt wonderful to be in the Sunshine State for a short and much-needed respite from the winter cold of New England. Our kids were so excited to be going to this beautiful theme park that we had told them about for months. Once inside, we began to make our way around to the various attractions.

One of the first places we came upon was a giant pirate ship that kids could climb on. Ben absolutely loved the ship and wanted to stay and play longer than the rest of us. We often found ourselves in a toe-to-toe battle with our kids wanting different things. We would accommodate Benjamin more than our other two—for obvious reasons. Michael and Jenna understandably carried resentment for that from the beginning. We decided it was time to move on from the ship. Ben resisted and resisted, but at last we broke him away from the pirate cove.

We were settling into the next exhibit when, much to my dismay, I realized my three-year-old boy was missing. I knew right where to find him, and sure enough, that little bugger defiantly found his way back to the pirate ship. Instead of making a scene, I called his dad and told him we would meet him shortly at a playground we had discovered —a safe play environment that gave parents a break. We were already exhausted and decided this would be a good place to hang out for a while to take a breather and let the kids do their thing.

Again, this was a safe, completely secure space for kids to play in, with parents perched outside the fence watching adoringly from the sidelines. Well, Benjamin managed to find in one of those fences a small opening that led to a beautiful, gigantic sand sculpture of Neptune. I remember someone saying, "Hey, whose kid is that?" Lo and behold, as Tom and I turned around, there was Ben—ready to pounce on it. This massive 1000-pound sand sculpture was one of many scattered throughout Sea World and took much effort and time to create. Tom screamed "**Stop!**" Thankfully, this was one of the few moments in our life when Ben actually listened. Phew! That was close. We continued on with our day, and for a while things went well.

Later in the afternoon, Ben spotted a small store with stuffed animals hanging from the roof. Of course, those toys cost $20 each and we had already spent a ton of money on many other things for our kids throughout the vacation. If we bought one, we would have to buy three, and it just wasn't in our budget. We told Ben that we would surprise him someday with a special one, but today we would have to say "no."

That was it! Ben went completely ballistic. Later, over the years, we learned more creative ways to say "no" to Ben, but in the early days, we hadn't discovered those finer parenting skills. In my upbringing and in Tom's family you just didn't ask because you knew the answer was an unequivocal "no." Clearly, saying "no" was not a big deal, since we had heard it most of our lives. With Benjamin, the word "no" was a huge button-pusher that usually turned into hours of screaming, begging, swearing and becoming completely out of control.

That day at Sea World, we as a family walked away from Ben. He followed behind us at a distance that felt safe for him. We kept our eyes on him, but left him with the idea that we were not going to be bullied into buying him something just because he wanted it. Suddenly, a family came up to him thinking he was lost, and we had to assure them that he was with us. So embarrassing! Imagine having your three-year-old child screaming and cursing at you for hours in a public place. If we had tried to pick him up and carry him out of there, we could have been accused of child abuse. It was an impossible situation, and beyond frustrating.

Eventually, we slowly made our way out of the park with Benjamin fighting us the whole way. Many times one of us would lose it and shake him or throw him with force into his car seat, to try to jolt him out of his mood. Any form of force only made him react more strongly.

So imagine now, eight years later, still dealing with the same scene—only now, Ben at eleven is much stronger and harder to control. One day we were heading to my sister Susan's for a visit. My sister Lyndsey was with me, along with my three children. Immediately upon getting into the car Ben asked for a hamburger. The kids had already had a snack, and we planned to eat lunch in New Hampshire with Susan and her boys. Of course, after years of dealing with these daily episodes, I had learned to make things very clear in order to avoid Ben's outbursts. Sometimes it worked, and sometimes it didn't. This particular day it didn't. As soon as I started driving, Ben went into an incessant dialogue of begging for what he wanted. Most of the time we tried to ignore him. However, once he was engaged, there was really no way out! As a family we tried everything.

I discovered through years of therapy that when Ben went into this behavior, he was in what I called a "brain-lock." It wasn't until he was completely spent and emotionally exhausted that his mind would finally relent and he would fall into a puddle of remorse. It was so hard to witness—and even harder to find solutions that would help him.

During this particular brain-lock, Ben actually threatened to jump out of the moving vehicle on a major interstate highway if we didn't give in to his plea. He suddenly opened the slider door while I was cruising along at 65 miles per hour. Lyndsey never had children of her own, but she describes this moment as an instinctual response that came instantaneously out of her. She said her arm swung across him, like the bionic woman, and she pulled him safely inside, slamming the door closed with her other arm. Michael and Jenna were in absolute terror, and Lyndsey told me to pull over at the nearest police station, which I did. We often found ourselves in front of police stations—and many times inside of them. Somehow, simply the sight of the station or the presence of a police officer would bring Benjamin out of his brain-lock, which it did then. (Just so you know, he didn't get his hamburger.)

I have often been accused of being too easy on my kids. My response over the years has been, "Really!" People thought that the reason I was dealing with a brain-locking child every day was because I said "yes" to everything he wanted. I absolutely had to choose my battles, and given the circumstances, anyone would most likely have done the same thing. Not only were these episodes daily, but they were also extremely volatile, frightening and seemingly unresolvable.

Michael learned early on to keep himself at an arm's length from Ben. He loved his brother, but became hugely independent early in his life—first and foremost to meet his own personal needs, and secondly to take the pressure off his mom. I am not sure I would have survived those early years with Benjamin had it not been for Michael's undeniable support and compassion for all those around him, especially me.

You can only imagine what life must have been like for Jenna, born almost exactly two years after her brother Ben. From the moment we brought her home from the hospital, Ben let it be known that she was not to thrive, shine or have her own space without his approval. They were both born in the sun sign of the ram, and rams they were. They butted heads from the moment Jenna joined our family. As tough as she was, Jenna wasn't strong enough to win against Benjamin's immovable energy. She tried her entire life to find the way through that wall of impossibility. They spent years fighting over everything from who got the front seat to what show they were watching on TV, and from whose friend was whose to the claim of ownership for just about anything around them. They were practically impossible. I used to say the biggest difference between Ben and Jen was that you could change Jenna's channel. Eventually, both came to a loving acceptance of one another—just months before Ben's death.

I have no doubt in my mind that there is a tremendous unraveling of karma present in the lives and lessons of Ben and Jenna. I only hope they are both able to clear that slate once and for all in this lifetime. Perhaps Ben's passing is now providing that opportunity for them both. However, it is not my karma or responsibility to ensure that reality. I have had my own karmic unraveling from the lifetime of challenge that I faced raising Ben. I am grateful and very proud to say that as difficult as it was, I did, in fact, clear the slate of past indiscretions and move beyond lifetimes of drama, blame and unresolved circumstances—all through the power of forgiveness.

At this point in the story, however, years of conventional therapy, medications and behavior techniques could not penetrate this insanity. Our lives were falling apart on a daily basis and we were becoming more and more separate from the world around us. Family and friends found it difficult to be in our presence. As much as they loved us, they couldn't help us. There had to be another solution. A piece was missing.

3

SARAH AND JACOB

Thankfully, through all this turmoil I was able to keep myself grounded. I depended on a daily practice of prayer, a deep and abiding faith with no particular religious base, amazing support from my sister Lyndsey and two close friends, Anne and Cynthia, along with my foundation of yoga and song circle, which I practiced weekly. I was able to stay connected enough to hear the voices of angels as they came through in many miraculous ways.

One of these miracles was an energy healer named Rose who amazingly showed up in my life at just the right time. Rose was a gift from God. She moved into my home and began the process of examining the patterns that created this insanity with Benjamin. It very quickly became obvious to me that the changes I sought for him began with me. We found that the archetypes of the victim, the wounded child and the attached-to-the-outcome seeker were being mirrored through my child's behaviors. If there was any hope for this family, my husband and I needed to focus our attention inward.

Our journey to discover the deep-seated karmic strand that had held our family in absolute chaos for twelve years began to unfold when we finally pulled Benjamin from the mainstream school system and attempted to home school him.

He was taking Prozac at this point and had become overweight from the medicine, seemingly lazy, and depressed. His self-esteem had reached an all-time low and his brain-locks—although less frequent because of the huge doses of medicine that he was prescribed—were doozies when they did happen. He was now much bigger and harder to control when he went into a tirade. He was also having great difficulty fitting in with his peers, although he did have a good friend named Alex who did his best to accept Ben as he was. This wasn't always easy, but Alex was a trooper.

To connect Ben and Jenna with other kids, we enrolled them in a wonderful after-school program called the Telamon Community Center at a local church. I was the creative director for the program and offered YogaKids classes and expressive art for the couple dozen kids who came there. My dear friend Anne and my son Michael, who was only fifteen at the time, worked for the program, too. It seemed to be a great place for us to find acceptance and to connect with other families who had kids that were also sensitive, creative and artistic. Ben had his good days and bad days at the Telamon Center, but since the people closest to him were part of the program, he was more accepted than he had been anywhere else. As his mother I was constantly walking on eggshells, knowing full well that at any moment Ben could have a meltdown or brain-lock and turn a fun-filled afternoon into a huge drama.

I also knew it would only be a matter of time before we would have to find a more permanent solution to our challenges as a family—even if that meant Benjamin had to live somewhere else for a while. Just the thought of it made me cry. Even though he was beyond difficult, I loved him more than words could express, and I didn't want to have to send him away. When Rose agreed to move in to our home and help us, I had renewed hope.

One day, as I was leaving the after-school program with Jenna, Ben completely freaked out. I don't even remember the specifics. All I know is that he wanted something I could

26

not give him. He started to bully me, swear at me, and make threats to Jenna and me. I just got into my van and drove away. Ben had his bike at the school and, unbeknownst to Jenna and me, he jumped on it immediately after we drove off, heading home in a rage after us. When he got home, he grabbed a plastic baseball bat from the yard and proceeded to beat my brand new mini-van with it. By the time the police arrived from my 911 call, he had put over twenty dents in my vehicle.

The police did what they had done on many other occasions in the past: they called an ambulance and had him transported to a local hospital for evaluation. By the time Benjamin got to the ER, he was out of his rage and had easily convinced the therapist on duty that he was fine. We learned early on that services for mental and emotional health issues were tremendously limited. At this point in Ben's life, we had been through the police, ambulance, and therapist routine enough times to know this route would get us nowhere. Later that evening, we sat down with Benjamin and told him he had to work with Rose every day for one hour, and that if we couldn't get him the help he needed, we would have to find a place that could. We all knew that we couldn't go on like this.

About two weeks later in one of Ben's sessions with Rose, she told him that she saw a past life in his auric field and asked his permission to reveal what she saw. Remember, Ben was only twelve years old at this time, and his response was, "I will do whatever it takes to understand what's wrong with me." He said, "I can't live like this anymore."

Rose told us that she saw Ben as a young man, about eighteen years old. His name was Jacob. He lived in the late 1700's on the very land where our current home sat. She said he had come across a British soldier in the woods near his home. The Revolutionary War had not yet begun, but Jacob was very angry. He had started a fight with the soldier and had stabbed him to death. That was all she saw.

Next, we decided to have Rose guide me into a past life regression to see if we could gain more insight. We learned in that session that I had been Jacob's mother. My name was Sarah Spencer. I originally lived in England. My husband Tom in this lifetime had been Sarah's father, who—back in England—was losing the castle he had inherited from his family. He decided to give his daughter Sarah (me) to a neighbor named George, who was taking his ship across the Atlantic Ocean to the New World. He thought he was providing her with a better life. Little did he know, as soon as the ship was out of sight George claimed Sarah as his slave bride. He raped her and beat her and moved her to a small farm in Massachusetts—on the very same land where we now live.

Sarah had two children: a son, Jacob (Benjamin), and a daughter, Jesse. When Jesse was a toddler, Sarah gave her away to a school teacher who came by in a wagon each day on her way to the nearby schoolhouse. Sarah wanted to save her daughter from the abuse in her home. Every day, especially when he was drunk, George abused his wife and children. Over time, as an escape from their miserable lives, Sarah and her son Jacob became drunks, too. When Jacob was sixteen years old, Sarah killed her abusive husband with rat poison.

Aha! Could this explain one of Benjamin's constant rituals? Ever since he could talk he would ask, "Am I going to get poisoned? Am I going to die?" As the past life regression continued, we learned that the night Jacob killed the soldier in the woods, he came home carrying a bloody knife, with blood all over his clothes. Sarah began to question her son and a fight broke out between them. They were both very drunk and tired of their pathetic existence. Sarah opened her arms to her son and said, "Go ahead. Kill me. I can't live like this anymore." Jacob then slit his mother's throat.

Did this new information explain why Benjamin as an infant, whenever he was within an arm's length of me, had his hand on my throat? This couldn't just be a coincidence.

Over the course of the next few months, my process to understand and make sense of what I had learned was beyond anything I could have imagined. The good news was that I now had something to work with. As out-of-the-box as this concept was, it was also the first thing that made any real sense. Now, every time Benjamin would go into one of his tirades, I would call Jacob out. At first, he would get very angry, but over time, Jacob began to lose power and Benjamin started to gain strength. The daily brain-locks became less frequent and life started to become more manageable. The more I addressed Jacob as a separate entity, the more he seemed to respond. It was quite miraculous.

One particular night, I was home alone with Ben. Rose was out for the evening and my other two kids were out with their dad. Benjamin, triggered by something, was suddenly in a major brain-lock. He had locked himself in his room with a book of matches and lighter fluid and was threatening to kill himself. He was screaming, "I can't do this anymore! I just want to die!" I sat outside his door trying to reason with him.

A year earlier, Ben's Uncle Larkin had passed to spirit. Larkin had been a strong presence in Ben's life both before and after his death. Ben called him his guardian angel. Ben had many angels, but Larkin was most special to him. I felt Larkin's energy in the room with Ben. Larkin was telling me to tell Ben to release Jacob to God. He said Jacob needed to be forgiven and sent to the light. I kept telling Ben what Larkin was saying. Ben was screaming: "I can't forgive him! He killed his mother!" I had already forgiven both Benjamin and Jacob in the months following my past-life regression, through healing work. Ben was aware of some of this process. I kept telling him through the door that I had forgiven them both and all he needed to do was to forgive Jacob and he would be free.

Finally, after about thirty minutes, I heard my son say those words out loud. He said, "Jacob, I forgive you. I send you to the light." Moments later the door opened. Benjamin and I sat in his room and wept.

Through this incredible process we were able to come to healing within ourselves and, in an instant, finally let go of the past. The years of family abuse ended on the night that Benjamin was finally able to release the energy that haunted him from the time he was born. Ben was able to send Jacob to the light through his ability to forgive and let go. It was by far the most miraculous moment I have ever witnessed. After twelve years of torment, we never saw the energy of Jacob again.

MICHAEL'S POEM

O Brother

I was a father
For a boy not even my own,
Too young to even fathom
What was wrong with him.
Jeckle and Hyde
Raged inside him
From the beginning of time
Until the night
When he released the demon to flight.
Until that night
Life was a gash that would never heal.
Until that night
We never cried so much all together.
Finally that night
I became your brother.

November 28, 2007

4

MOVING ON

"Miracle" doesn't even begin to describe the depth of relief I felt as Ben's mother after the release of Jacob's spirit to God. I remember for months bracing myself for the return of the brain-locks and behavioral outbursts that I had experienced for what felt like a lifetime. As each day passed, I became more and more certain that Jacob was in fact *gone!* For the next several years, Benjamin would tell us he saw Sarah's and Jacob's spirits waving to him on the side of the road whenever he drove by the farm where we lived in our past life, just around the bend from our present house.

Whatever transpired that night—whether it was a story that we created subconsciously to allow forgiveness to happen, or one that stemmed from actual events from a past life (and to me, it didn't really matter)—we were finally free. My son was finally healing and growing each day into a normal teenage boy.

He had his struggles, but he learned to deal with them more effectively. He shifted more easily, and over time he was usually easier to manage than my other two kids. He still had occasional brain-locks, but they were few and far between and did not last long. He also still suffered with OCD (Obsessive Compulsive Disorder) and anxiety, but the out-of-control behavior was a thing of the past. Ben came off of the 80 mgs of Prozac his therapist prescribed to a much lower dose. He lost weight through work with a trainer, went back to mainstream school, and began the process of healing and profound change.

School was a challenge for him both academically and socially. Teenagers are not very forgiving. It took him many years to overcome his past. He sat alone at the lunch table for the first two years of high school. Over time, though, Ben became more and more comfortable in his own skin. He had learned many tools from me to help him strengthen his sense of self.

He was now growing tall and handsome. The girls had started to notice him. After a lifetime of being left out, a beautiful girl invited him to his junior prom. It was all he could talk about.

He had also, by the grace of God, passed the MCA's (Massachusetts Comprehensive Assessment tests). When he came back to public high school in the ninth grade, he was finally tested to identify his learning challenges and assess his grade level. They discovered that his learning curves were huge and that he was academically behind four grade levels. Despite all his obstacles, however, he had found his way. At this juncture, he was just one year shy of graduating from high school. We were so proud of Ben for all he had overcome in his short life. He had such promise for his future.

Then on April 16, 2009, six days after his eighteenth birthday and nine days before his prom, Ben arrived at school with the smell of marijuana on his clothing. He was brought to the "powers that be" who proceeded to search his car. They found a small amount of marijuana and a pipe. Ben had been using marijuana to self-medicate. He also used it to help him fit in with his peers. We and his school therapist were aware of this. Marijuana seemed to be the only thing at this point that helped his OCD symptoms. And in January of that same year, the Massachusetts law decriminalizing marijuana had gone into effect. Ben was very aware of this.

However, the school administrators proceeded to hand over their punish-ment to Ben for possession of marijuana:

he was given three days suspension, a $100 fine and was prohibited from attending his prom. So here was this sensitive boy who had overcome so many social obstacles in his short life, having the rug pulled out from under his one success: social acceptance by his peers. Ben came home from school, and within thirty minutes of receiving his punishment, wrote a beautiful, loving note to his family and proceeded to hang himself in our garage. It is my belief that the emotional impact of losing his prom caused my son his final brain-lock. [See Chapter 17, The Perfect Storm, for the full story.]

Just months before, the school had witnessed Ben brain-locking when they wanted to give him detention for being late. He had brain-locked because he believed his reason for being late should have been excused. At first, the school therapist was not willing to shift the rules to accommodate him. After I explained brain-locking to him, we came up with a solution that helped Ben come out of the brain-lock. He was still held accountable for his actions, but in a different way which made more sense to him. He was then able to shift.

I wish that on the day he died the school had paused and considered the implication of their actions. We have come a long way as a society to recognize and support those dealing with *physical* disabilities; however, those with mental illness are still expected to follow the same rules as normal kids. My son had special needs. He was *not* one of the normal kids. Had we met with his team collectively before the authorities handed down that impulsive punishment, I am sure Ben would still be here with us today.

5

MY GREATEST LOSS

Ben's decision to end his life created a shock wave into the core of my being. I was completely devastated. After everything we had been through I could not believe this was how our journey would end.

The ceremony for honoring his life and his presence was tremendous—more than I could have ever imagined. Not only was this honoring a testament to the energy of this amazing young man, but also a testament to each of us, as individuals, within this family. The outpouring of love for all of us, the deep sadness felt by all who joined in the recognition of his passing, was and will always be a true blessing for which I am eternally grateful.

Ben was a Buddha in our midst, something I have always sensed and known. He had an extraordinary life. He was the most compassionate, loving, sensitive, and empathic being I have ever known. His presence, his smile and his bright eyes would light up an entire room. He felt other people's pain and had little to no tolerance for behaviors that were out of integrity. At times, his method for bringing others into accountability was fierce and difficult to receive. I had on many occasions met his fierceness head on, and hit an enormous, immovable wall of energy.

I learned, as his mother, to let go of my need to be right—to just love him and let him be. Later, we would talk things through, once the energy softened and he had let go completely and come back to the present moment. In the days following Ben's death, a statement exclaimed by a member of our family continued to ring in my ears: "Suicide is a permanent solution to a temporary problem."

Yesterday it hit me: those suffering with mental illness are dealing every day with challenges that most of us cannot understand. The problems are *not* temporary ones; they are constant, and Ben dealt with them every day like a champion. Please understand that I am not advocating for anyone who reads this to go out and end their life. Hopefully, this puts into perspective the astronomical challenges that this young man—and many others like him—face on a day-to-day basis. I have hope that through increased awareness we can find solutions to prevent this horrific outcome for others who suffer.

Those who knew Ben well were acutely aware of his continuous stream of rituals, which he hid from most of his community and peers. His fear of being judged, criticized, and misunderstood was his greatest challenge socially. Most of his peers had no idea of the inner demons he fought against every day. He didn't let anyone get too close—especially *girls!* If he let anyone get too close, he feared they would see his brokenness. From the stream of young women who attended his funeral, it was clear that there were many who would have loved the chance to get closer to him. He was physically gorgeous, but, of course, he thought he was ugly!

Within an educational system designed to serve only the average, normal child, Ben found learning to be painful and difficult. He agonized through every single day and came home with knots the size of grapes all along his scapula bones, which I lovingly called his "angel wings." We had a nightly ritual. "Mom," he would say, "can you *push* on my back?" I would stop whatever I was doing and massage him until all his "demons" from the day were released from his body. His sister, brother and closest friends were witness to this event on many occasions. Sometimes they would line up asking me to push on their backs, too. He would make sounds to help release his anguish, and I would sit on him and push, squeeze, knead and heal. This was yet another ritual in his life—one that I believe saved him for many years.

As a teacher, healer and spiritual seeker for the past fifteen years, I am now at peace with the loss of this immense presence who graced me with his life for eighteen short years. I understand now, and see the bigger picture; I know that as I move forward he will continue to be the inspiration for my work as a healer and teacher. Even this innate knowledge, though, does not bring solace to the deep vibrational tear of pain at the center of my heart as his mother. He knew I would be devastated. He also knew that he needed to take care of himself. To be true to oneself at the expense of others is not widely accepted here. In our society, we call the act of self-loving "selfish." It is my belief that this is the highest form of self-love.

Benjamin loved all of those around him deeply. His suicide was filled with love and concern for those he was leaving behind him. There was no anger, no judgment, no guilt or shame—just a clear sense of surrender to release his pain and suffering. From the moment Ben passed to spirit, I have felt, seen and heard his presence. His *being-ness* is larger than life, his spirit is soaring, his body is empty, and a mere shell of what was once a boy carrying the spirit of a master. His presence in human form will be missed beyond words. His spirit lives on in my heart, mind, memories and choices. I am so grateful for the gift of being his mother. He was one of my greatest teachers, and I will hold him close in my heart until my own dying day.

6

IN JENNA'S WORDS

It was just a normal day. I was awakened by a phone call around 11:00 a.m. from my mom telling me that my brother got suspended and was not answering her calls. She wanted me to find him. I got up, not thinking anything of it, and went outside and saw my brother's bright blue car. I called him about ten times, texted him at least five. His not answering got me worried, so I started looking outside, screaming his name. I checked his car and it was unlocked. My brother Ben suffered from Obsessive Compulsive Disorder (OCD) which is an illness that causes you to obsess over little things, so his car doors being unlocked never *ever* happened. That's when I knew something was wrong.

I ran in the house and found the worst letter I've ever read. It was from Ben. On the front, he wrote: "Goodbye Family, I Love You." On the inside was a very, sad, rushed goodbye letter. After I read it, I knew he was gone. But I still had hope! I ran outside and met my mom, who was just pulling into the driveway. I showed her the letter, and automatically, she called 911. As she was looking for him, I don't know why, but I had a sudden urge to look in the garage. So, I opened it slowly, hoping it wasn't true—but there I found my brother. He died from suicide.

On April 16, 2009 my life changed a hundred percent. Before this day, my life was great! I had everything I ever wanted. In my head, I honestly thought I would have my family forever.

Ben's death has completely changed me as a person. I am constantly letting my family and friends know how much I love them. I know I could lose anyone, any day, so I don't take my life for granted. The loss of my brother was so random; I never thought I would lose my brother that unexpectedly. His death changed my whole life, family and friends. I never got to say goodbye. The night before he died, we said goodnight, and he told me he loved me. Little did I know, I'd wake up and he'd be dead. I still miss him to this day.

My family and I are working to educate others and stop teen suicide and depression. The loss of my brother impacted my family so deeply that we want to help other families struggling the same way we did. We created the non-profit organization called Ben Speaks Louder Than Words. My mom speaks in schools here and wants to speak all over the world to tell her story, and to give kids positive solutions to their problems without using drugs and alcohol or being depressed. I hope my family and I can help change the world with our story.

7

THE TIP OF THE ICEBERG

The days following the loss of my son Benjamin have been filled with a tremendous amount of synchronicity that has left me feeling in complete awe of this three-dimensional-experience called life on planet Earth. My personal healer has been a steady voice of support through my process of this loss. Some of her early bits of wisdom to me were to stay in the flow. Let go of control. Be present as much as possible. I know from my own work over the past many years that our greatest suffering comes from our attachments.

In my own case, I have witnessed my own attachment to my son, to his life that I cannot bring back, to my wanting—so desperately, as his grieving mother—to bring him back. I want to reclaim the memories of his life—a life that was swept away by a decision made in a fleeting moment. There truly is *no* wrongness in anything we choose; however, there is consequence. Sometimes those consequences affect many of us on a larger scale. This leaves many of us feeling angry or filled with a feeling of victimization. Ben's loss is an example of that. Moving forward, my own decisions are an opportunity for me to choose wisely—not only for myself, but also for the betterment of my two surviving children, my husband and all of those within my sphere of influence.

Ben's memorial service was so beautiful and was inspired by Spirit. Spirit moved through me, my amazing sister Lynn, my husband Tom, and many others who brought pieces of divine teaching, sharing, and love to every moment of our celebration of him. The impact of Ben's life has touched many, many people and continues to inspire and create healing far beyond our moment of tribute and release of his spirit to God.

Two days after the memorial, Lynn, Tom and I were invited to find solace, space and respite in the arms of a very loving and present woman. I had recently met her through my women's networking group, the Dream Factory Community. Nancy was amazing. We went to her humble, yet lovely abode on the North Shore of Massachusetts. She nurtured us with delicious food, a great listening ear, and a tremendous view of the harbor—well beyond the setting of the sun. It was magical and peaceful. As we became chilled by the nighttime ocean air, we retreated into her warm house.

The house was dimly lit, and Nancy and I began to speak about Spirit. She shared with me about the loss of her father, to whom she was very close. She felt sad that it was difficult to connect with his spirit. One of my own gifts as a healer and teacher is the ability to channel Spirit. I have been developing myself as a spirit medium for many years, and teach others to develop this gift which is accessible—with practice—to all of us. That night I was able to bring her a clear message of her father's presence in the room with us. She was moved by this and was grateful. We then joined Lynn and Tom in the living space. The room was very quiet.

My sister Lynn possessed a similar gift of channeling Spirit, though her gift was through her singing voice. While chatting with Tom in the living room she was inspired to sing and wasn't sure why. When Nancy and I walked into the living room and shared our moment in the kitchen with Lynn and Tom, Lynn was now very clear about Spirit's communication to sing. Nancy was open to this beautiful, organic and inspired message. Lynn sang about an iceberg. It was a brilliant aqua blue, jutting out like a pyramid above the surface of the ocean. A whale and a seal were swimming around the iceberg. They brought a message for each of us. For me, a picture began to form in my head. Because I am a visual and kinesthetic learner, my imagination immediately took me to the whale. Through her, I felt myself diving deep into the ocean. I began to reflect on the enormity of the iceberg beneath the surface. This whale was taking me on a journey to the depths of the vast ocean beneath my own thoughts. It was yet another reminder for me to look deeper than what my mind has been taught, to reveal the deeper truths of life.

Ben's loss has been a catalyst for me to really dig deep, to go to the well or vast ocean of faith within me—the deeper knowing that transcends the fear of my mind; to remember God and grace, forgiveness, love and acceptance. It has caused me to remember that my mind is merely the tip of the iceberg, and to go beneath the surface to my voice—so beautifully represented by the whale singing her heart song through Lynn. It reminded me to transcend my fears by connecting to the joy and playful opportunity of life, as represented by the seal. How I choose to move forward through my pain will be a living memorial to my son's life. I thank all the players on the stage of life that day for this important teaching.

8

IT IS THE CIRCLE

People have often asked me, "What do you mean by 'connecting the dots'?" This was the tag line of my company at the time, "Circle Works." I will attempt to explain here.

It has been two weeks since the passing of my son Benjamin, but he is not completely lost to me. He has been communicating with me since the moment of his passing. His spirit was with me during my morning walk today, helping me to put into perspective the deeper meaning of the choices we have all made up to this point, in what we humans know as time.

Many years ago, we were visiting my sister Susan, way up in the northern part of New Hampshire. Michael was only eight years old and had never experienced a nosebleed. That morning he awoke covered in blood. Tom and I were freaked out because we had been watching too many episodes of "The X-Files" on television; our imagination had gotten the better of us since we knew that sometimes nosebleeds were associated with alien abduction. After a few weeks passed, we let it go.

About a year later, Michael awoke to another nosebleed. Our alarm clock showed that our power had gone off at around 4:00 a.m. At that time, my sister Candace lived upstairs in a separate apartment, and she too had lost power. No one else on the street had lost power that night. Many alien shows over the years have spoken of a connection between nosebleeds and power going off. Once again, my fears took over as my central nervous system kicked into high gear. I went for a very long walk to have one of my many conversations with God. I remember screaming out into the universe, *"What am I supposed to do with this?"* The only thing I heard in that moment was a voice in my head saying, "See the love in it." From that moment on, I let go of all fear and shifted my thinking to believe that this was Michael's process, and somehow it would lead him back to love. If he needed to connect in some way to aliens to bring good to the world, then so be it! I guess you would have to ask Michael for his take on this experience. For me, it was another opportunity to surrender to love—to let go and let God.

Several nights later, I awoke after remembering a dream about crop circles. I spent a few days researching them on the Internet. For at least a year I'd been singing in a song circle with my sister Lynn, where we gathered together a circle of friends joining in to sing one inspired song at a time. Now I was beginning to see the circles of people starting to surface all around me from a more awakened state of mind.

A very simple song then channeled through me, and the concept of *circle* became very clear to me. The song goes like this:

> *It is the circle where power lies.*
> *It is the circle where strength resides.*
> *It is the circle where faith can grow.*
> *It is the circle that makes us whole.*
> *Join hands together and live as one,*
> *Where every person shares their own love.*
> *Join hands together, let goodness grow.*
> *It is the circle that makes us whole.*

So here I am, once again reflecting on the circle. When Ben made the decision to take his life, his death created a shockwave that touched many, many people. I see the shockwave as a circle. I also see the community that emerged through this shock as a circle of family and support. In our direct sphere of influence, at least a thousand lives were affected. Through it I felt and witnessed an outpouring of love that was so beautiful. I remember wondering, "Why must we have a tragedy like this to know how much we are loved?"

In that circular shockwave I saw a side of people that I had never seen before. It was incredibly wonderful. Ben's death created healing on so many levels. I saw my husband's family, after years of conflict, put aside their differences to support their brother. I came full circle with my own brother after twenty years of separation. Many of the energetic threads of unresolved issues with others completely melted away. I witnessed a greater awareness of mental illness and a willingness of many to embrace the conversations of change in moving forward. I felt loved by a community that up until Ben's death seemed distant and uncaring. My daughter Jenna, after taking herself out of high school—based on school phobia and severe anxiety after being ostracized and bullied since her return to public school in the eighth grade —made a decision to re-enter high school the following year. This would not have happened had she not felt the outpouring of love from those who had once treated her badly.

I began to ask myself, "Why are so many children choosing to take their lives at this time on our planet?" I recently read a report which said that *twenty-eight children every week* are leaving us by choice—not to mention the thousands that go unreported or are unsuccessful attempts. I am always open to seeing the bigger picture. I believe that

that we each have a role to play in bering who we are. We are so much d minds; at our core we are love. her suicides are acting as a message back to love? What if their purpose ear consciousness?

49

The way I see it, our world is experiencing brain-lock. Ben spent his whole life living with Obsessive Compulsive Disorder. Brain-lock happened when he got stuck on a thought process and was not able to let it go—at times, for hours. When he was younger he would literally be willing to fight to his death for whatever was stuck in his head. Over time and with maturity he learned to tone it down, but it was still a part of his daily process. As my sister Lynn said in Ben's eulogy, we believe he brain-locked on the day he decided to release himself from this life.

Perhaps this was the very tool this young master in our midst needed in order to follow through with his script. What if his sole purpose in life was to bring this as a mirror to the forefront? Or, what if it was to show us the extreme set of circumstances we find ourselves in as a society? We live in a world of unlimited possibilities, and yet most of us cannot see beyond what we know. Maybe it is time for us to let go of what we have created thus far . . . to throw in the towel, so to speak, and come, full circle, back to our hearts. Or, at least, to let go of what is clearly not working and trust in our hearts that new possibilities will emerge in the process. What would happen if all our actions and choices came from our hearts and not our heads? Anyone who knew Ben well saw this dichotomy being played out in living color. He was either stuck in his head to the point of being unmovable, or on the opposite polarity: so open to love that it hurt him deeply. His empathy was remarkable.

My gift as a teacher and healer is to see the bigger picture, to connect the dots from my experiences, making a circle that embraces greater learning. I can see that all of my life experiences, as frightening and devastating as they may feel in the moment, continue to connect me back to my heart. Whether placing his right hand over his heart in a gesture love, or hugging you to the right side to connect heart was known to say to many who knew him, "Heart

I am forever grateful for the lessons bestowed upon me by all of those within my circle of influence. I hope that Ben's lessons and teachings will also bring greater awareness to the others within those circles of shockwaves from his death.

Benjamin was a true master and student on this beautiful round planet, and I honor him for his gifts and his willingness to sacrifice his life to teach us. Let Ben's passing be the last of our children to attempt to teach us these lessons. I pray that we are able to come back to our loving hearts, love and accept each other's differences, find peaceful solutions to our suffering, and finally come full circle back to love—as a world community.

9

THE PHOENIX RISING

While losing Ben has been the greatest challenge and most amazing experience of my life, I have spent the last ten weeks since his death in complete amazement, awe, acceptance, grace, guidance and deep grief. I feel like I am living in two different realities simultaneously—which is part of the experience of living in a world of opposites in this life school called Planet Earth.

On one hand I am a mother, grieving deeply for the loss of this beautiful, empathic, creative, energetic, lost boy of the world. I miss the sound of his loud and present voice bouncing through my kitchen each day saying, "Hey Maaa! What's up?" I miss the touch of his arms finding solace in my loving embrace when his day felt too heavy to carry. I miss the daily routine of pushing on his stressed-filled body to release, through sound, his empathic absorption of the world's suffering. I miss the touch of his short haircut, like a soft ball of fuzz. I miss that *so* much! Mostly, I miss his beaming smile and huge energy! I even miss how impossible he could be and how he took up more than his share of space in my home, car or any place we happened to be.

On the other hand, I spent the first twelve years of his life trying to fit him into a structure that didn't serve him. Finally, after years of trial and error, immersed in what felt, at times, like a very messy petri dish of life in the Gio household, I learned to respect his space, trust his process, and treat him as the aware and conscious being that he was. Ben pushed all the buttons: mine, his father's, his siblings' and those of anyone else who, for their own learning, fell onto his path.

I have said before that Ben has been and continues to be my greatest teacher. My relationship with him has now shape-shifted into something much bigger than my mind could even fathom. From the moment I witnessed his lifeless shell on the gurney in the hospital, I have felt his presence and heard his voice, led by his spirit. Immediately upon entering the hospital room, he told me to get ready to embark on a journey together that was planned long before either of us incarnated into the Earth plane. He assured me that nothing could have stopped the events that came together to create "the perfect storm" for his "stage-left exit." He said it was my destiny to become a voice for change *through him* and that the name of the organization we would create together was going to be called Ben Speaks Louder Than Words. In the early stages of witnessing this, I thought I was making it all up in my head.

That same afternoon of his death, myriads of family, friends, colleagues and healers began to surround me. I was immediately scooped onto a healing table in the early hours of the day by a friend who is a gifted massage therapist. As I lay on the table, my naked body broken open with grief, I asked Ben to give me a sign that he was still with me. I saw in my third eye a vision of Ben as a giant winged light being coming down from above and wrapping me like a cocoon in his loving wings. My sobbing, aching, heartbroken body was able to release my early grief into his loving embrace. He was giving back to me what I had done for him for years. Moments later, I saw him as Ben, taking my hand and bringing me to a giant ball of light. He kept saying, "Look at this, Mom! You've got to see this! It's amazing!"

After this cathartic massage session, I went downstairs to the new wave of folks coming to share in our loss, and my husband took his turn on the healing table with Beth. Later we learned that Tom experienced *the same vision* during his healing. He had asked Ben to come to him and help him with his grief. Tom's description was the same as mine.

Several hours later, my friend and colleague Lisa Campion, a gifted healer, teacher, psychic and medium, came to see me. She told me that over the years in her healing practice she has connected with many people who have been involved with suicide. She told me that Ben's death was very different from most suicides she had witnessed. According to Lisa, he left with purpose—no karmic threads, clear and clean. He left his body with the greatest of ease and release, and said that he was a "Rising Phoenix." Since then I have seen Ben in my mind's eye almost like an opaque Academy Award statue with giant wings.

Recently, I saw Lisa again for a healing session and psychic reading. I hadn't seen her since she came to my house the day Ben died. As soon as I laid down on the table, she told me Ben's presence was in the room. She described him as a giant statue-like bird with enormous wings. The first thing he asked her to say to me was, "Hey Ma, can you give me a little credit now for how hard it was for me to fit into that itty bitty costume for as long as I did?" My answer to him in that moment was, "I got it, Buddy. Say no more!"

Since my healing with Lisa, the messages have become even stronger. We are in constant dialogue. I asked Ben the day before I wrote this essay to show me a sign that I was on the right path (as though he hadn't given me enough signs already!). I looked up into the sky after we had had twenty-eight solid days of rain. The sky was bright blue with big, white puffy clouds that morphed into all kinds of shapes when I watched them. I kept my eye on one particular cloud for a few moments as I was walking along. Before I knew it, the cloud changed itself into the shape of a phoenix rising! I came home and sat down at my computer, preparing to document my experience of the past twenty-four hours. I opened my email, reading about the latest crop circle discovered in England on June 12, 2009, about two months after Ben's death. (Remember, I had been fascinated by crop circles many moons before.) I'll bet you can guess what the crop circle was. Yup! You got it! It was *a phoenix rising!*

10

SIGNPOSTS ALONG THE WAY

Losing a child has got to be the most painful experience that any human being must endure. I can honestly say that my heart is broken in a million pieces. I am completely and utterly grateful for the stream of signs I have received from my son's spirit since his passing. He has provided me with continuous reminders that our spirit lives on and is never completely separate from us. It is my belief that the body is a vehicle for our spirit to experience a series of life lessons, and once we have completed our mission, we leave our bodies and return home to the Eternal One. Although my son is no longer in body, he is clearly still here.

The first sign of Ben's communicating with me in physical form was the appearance of coins placed precisely where I would find them. Several nights after Ben passed, my sister Lyndsey decided to call together a group of women from her song circle days. Many women joined us to sing our heart songs for Ben, to support me in my process of grief and loss, and to reconnect to their sisters in song. One of the women in our group told me that Ben had come to her. She said he told her that he would let me know he was still with me by giving me quarters. That evening, as I prepared to go to sleep, I pulled back the sheets on my bed and there in the center lay my first quarter from heaven! I received many more in the days following. I would find them in my car, placed perfectly centered on my seat, in the dryer, on my night stand—always a single quarter placed strategically so I would find it. I have come to know over the years as a psychic and medium that Spirit will always find a way to communicate through whatever is recognizable to the person still on earth. I wasn't surprised that Benjamin would choose the larger of our familiar coins. He always wanted the best of everything; a penny or a dime just wasn't good enough!

I would lie in bed at night wondering what other methods Benjamin would use to communicate with me. I have always identified with animals and have received many messages throughout my life from animal spirits. I decided that if Ben showed himself to me in the form of an animal, it would either be a cow or a turtle. Both of these animals were significant in our lives.

Several days after Ben's funeral, we left for Florida to give ourselves some much-needed space to heal and to reconnect as a family of four. We invited Mike's friend Chris and Jenna's friend Maddie to join us. Once settled in our timeshare, we began the new journey of life without Ben. As you can imagine, there was now a giant hole in the fabric of our family. I wanted desperately to feel him, hear his voice, and see his presence in some way, shape or form.

One night before going to bed, I asked his spirit to bring me a sign. I was awakened at 5:30 the next morning by the sound of his voice in my head. He said, "Mom, get up." A little annoyed by the time of day, I told him to get back to me later. Some things never change. Ben, as he was here on Earth, was still very persistent in the spirit world. He continued to nudge me out of bed. At 6:15, I heard him say again, "Mom, get up, you're going to miss it." That was all I needed to hear. I dragged myself out of bed, threw on some clothes and my sneakers, and decided to go outside. I went through the back porch to keep from waking my sleeping teens. Just before swinging the door open, I noticed a presence there. Sitting so close to the screen that his beak nearly touched it was a huge duck. I bent down, and said

"Hey, what's up, duck?" Moments later, tears flew to my eyes! It took a moment for me to register the significance of a *duck* at my doorstep. Of course, Benjamin would show himself as a duck! How could I forget? He loved talking like Donald Duck from the time he was a kid until his dying day. I ran inside yelling, "It's Benjamin! It's Benjamin! He came to visit us!" My sleepy teens began to drag themselves out of bed, along with their dad.

Pictures, tears, amazement, gratitude and genuine connection were the order of the day for the next hour. We hung out with our duck until we were satisfied. He just waddled around, happy to be with us, and even happier to receive some breakfast from Jenna. Then we noticed that *the duck had a wound all the way around his neck.* If you recall, Benjamin had hung himself.

The kids decided it was still too early to continue the day, and back to bed they went. I was so jazzed and wide awake that I chose to go for a walk instead. This time, I left through the front door. Not more than a hundred feet along the road, sitting in the middle of a giant puddle in the center of the street was . . . you guessed it—another duck! Ben had me covered at both ends. This duck was threatening to fly away from the moment I encountered him. He had been waiting there for some time, I am sure. I fiddled with my phone, desperately trying to figure out how to take this second duck's picture. I begged Ben to find a way to keep the duck there until I mastered my picture-taking capability. The duck continued to flap his wings, but stayed in place. Finally, I figured it out and said, "Okay, ducky, now you can shake your tail feathers." And lo and behold, he gave me a full wing span. Those were the only two ducks I encountered on the entire vacation.

Several days later, we went to visit my cousin Diane in Amelia Island, on the northeast coast of Florida. From the time we arrived until the day we left, the island was pummeled by a storm. It was dramatically windy and wild, with immense waves crashing on the beach. I remember thinking, "What are the chances of encountering such an intense storm on a beach and an island that, according to my cousin, was beautiful and sunny 363 days of the year?" Rather than choosing (as my kids did) to feel slighted by Mother Nature, I chose to see the raw power and excitement of the storm and felt gifted by its presence. It helped me feel closer to Ben.

One afternoon, Tom, Diane, her little boy and I decided to take a walk in a nearby park and left the teens at home with a movie. This park was one of the most beautiful places I have ever been. We ventured into the rain and wind, and journeyed through a set of trails that circled around a moss-filled pond. I suddenly noticed the sound of several bullfrogs. They became louder and louder. I said to my cousin, "It's funny. I asked Ben to show himself to me today, and I wonder if the bullfrogs are him." Ben was one of the loudest people I have ever known. His voice was booming and powerful. As soon as I acknowledged that I recognized it was him, all of the bullfrogs stopped croaking at the exact same time. It seemed just too synchronized to be a coincidence. Again, I felt I had been blessed by Ben's presence.

We still had several days left in Florida, and spent many days scouting around the Orlando area, taking the kids to see the sights, visiting local beaches and rummaging through the myriad of stores in the area. One day, we stopped at a flea market. I needed to use the restroom and told the gang I would find them later. I started off to find the nearest bathroom.

Years ago, when my father died, he gifted me with his only special possession in life. It was a black onyx elephant with ivory tusks—the last remaining of many artifacts his mother had brought back from the Orient in her travels as a young woman. Mind you, I am the fifth child of six—not to mention a girl. I thought fathers passed family heirlooms on to their sons. I was perplexed at the time and thought it was quite odd for my father to choose me as the ambassador of his sole prize possession. Anyway, I held onto this elephant for years.

At the time my father died, my brother Mark was the black sheep of the family, and did not join his siblings for his father's funeral. One day, while sitting in meditation on my front porch, I received a direct channel from what felt like angels speaking through me. I transcribed a letter to my brother with clear instructions from above to send this letter to him—along with the elephant. The letter was about giving the burdens of the past to the elephant through forgiveness. A year later my grandmother died at the age of 98, and, by the grace of God, Mark showed up in upstate New York for her memorial. After fifteen years, my mother finally had all six of her children in the same room. The first thing Mark said to me when we saw each other was, "Thank you for the elephant." That's all he needed to say for me to know that it was impactful. The elephant had brought him home.

Since then, I have stopped at every shop I've encountered where carved elephants with tusks of bone (no longer ivory) are displayed. I wanted to replace the elephant that my father gifted to me, since I gave his elephant to Mark. Here I was, in this flea market, having finally located the restroom, when I came upon a huge shop filled with African carvings. The shop owner immediately walked over to me. He told me he had been carving things since he was three years old. He was deeply moved by the story of my search for the perfect elephant, and by the loss of my son from suicide. Before I knew it, he had found for me the perfect carved elephant.

Upon my return from the restroom, I saw Tom at the register preparing to pay for the elephant. The shop owner was telling Tom a story as I walked up. He said he was a visionary and had brought many messages to his customers over the years. He reflected back on his most recent vision. A year ago, he had told a woman that she was going to have a daughter in the month of September—after many, many years of her not being able to get pregnant. He told the woman to come back and tell him if his vision came to pass. Days before our encounter with him, the woman visited him with her baby girl, who had been born just as he said, in September. He said he needed to tell us this story so we would know he was credible and gifted in his ability to see the future.

He then turned directly to me. He looked deep into my eyes and gave me the following message: "You have been struggling for a very, very long time. You have been trying desperately to pull others toward you to share your gifts with the world. You are now coming into much good luck. The days of struggle are over. I see you on a platform and many, many people are coming to hear you. You are coming into much good fortune." To which my husband replied, "Oh, you see her on Oprah, too?" Another signpost from Spirit!

After our return from Florida, life became more difficult. The hundreds of people who came to support us through our tragic loss began to fade into the woodwork. We were now back to the day-to-day of life without Ben. Each of the four of us needed to find the strength within ourselves to live without this missing piece that had taken so much space within our world for so long. The more time passed, the deeper we felt our grief. Of course, this had to be the summer we received thirty days of continuous rain. Try going through grief with a constant blanket of darkness all around you. It was tough!

Feeling more and more disconnected from Benjamin, I was desperate to feel his presence once again. On this particular evening, I was scheduled to attend the yearly conference of the Dream Factory Community, a local networking group for women entrepreneurs. I decided to go to get out of the house and to reconnect with some of the amazing women with whom I have networked over the years. The conference started on Friday night and ended the following afternoon. Most years, I stayed the night, but this year I decided to go home. It was raining, or shall I say, pouring buckets all the way home. I called home to check in with Tom, and he shared with me a new realization. He had been looking carefully at Ben's suicide note and noticed that Ben had written it and then folded it in half. On the back side of the note were the last words ever written by my beautiful boy. He wrote, "Good Bye Family, I love you!" That evening, I cried and cried and cried! And the world cried with me as the rain fell throughout the night to meet me in my pain.

The next day, I dragged myself out of bed and went back to the conference. I asked Ben to show himself to me that morning before I left. I was running late and knew I had missed the breakfast they served, so I pulled into Honey Dew Donuts to get a croissant. At the time, I hadn't thought of the significance of Honey Dew Donuts. Ben used to be addicted to the blueberry donuts there and would have meltdowns on many occasions if I didn't stop to get him one. So here I was, pulling through the drive-thru at Honey Dew Donuts, waiting for my order, when out of the corner of my eye I saw a huge snapping turtle crossing the curb onto the pavement right next to me. There was my sign! It was the turtle I had been waiting for since Ben's passing.

For many years, whenever Ben was upset or scared, he would pull his shirt over his head and say, "I am going in my turtle shell." To him, it represented protection. He and I also saved a snapping turtle on the side of the road a few years back. Now this turtle, two feet from my car, had his head facing away from me. I rolled down my passenger side window and prepared my cell phone to snap a picture. I said to the turtle, "Thank you, son, so much, for showing yourself to me today." In that moment, the turtle turned and looked directly at me.

Life goes on without Ben. I still miss him so much! Several months have drifted by. I am now taking a long weekend to beautiful Star Island, off the coast of New Hampshire and Maine for a yoga retreat with my yoga trainer. It is raining once again. I arrive at Rye Beach early, with an hour to kill before catching the ferry to the island. I walk down to the beach in hopes of connecting to Ben in some way. Standing along the edge of the rock-covered beach, I hear Ben's voice telling me to look for heart rocks. Within minutes, I find a large rock, perfectly formed in the shape of a heart. I placed this gem in my car and hear him say to go back. He tells me I will find two more. Believe it or not, within ten minutes I find two more beautiful heart rocks.

Whenever I am in the pit of despair and deep grief which is the inevitable partner to such momentous loss, I ask Ben to show me a physical sign that his presence is still with me. It is in those darkest moments that the magic of his beautiful essence comes through in miraculous ways. Yesterday, I found myself in such a state of deep grief that I thought my heart was going to completely shatter into pieces. I gave myself permission to really feel the depth of my pain. I know this is healthy and wise and will prevent me from falling into not only a deep pit of despair, but also depression. I have learned to feel my feelings.

Once again I ask Ben for a sign, and within minutes receive a call from my sister Lyndsey—all the way from Arizona. She asks me if I was in a state of deep grief today. I said," Yes, just minutes ago!" She says, "I knew it! I was driving to church just moments ago and suddenly was completely enveloped by a blanket of deep grief and was sobbing uncontrollably. I knew it didn't belong to me. I knew it had to be you." I tell her I had just asked Ben for a sign that he was still with me. She replies immediately, "And here it is! Remember little sister, we are all connected."

11

ANOTHER SIGNPOST

Over the past several months I have connected with many people who have lost their children or someone they love as a result of varying tragedies. We are losing our children to cancer, freak accidents, suicide, accidental overdoses, drunk driving and even the flu. Everyone seems to be touched by loss in some way. Many who have experienced such loss are unable to connect in any way to their loved ones.

Although my life has been shattered in many ways, there are frequent moments in my life where I feel truly blessed. I ask myself, "Am I special?" I know the answer to that question already. No one is more special than anyone else. We are all equal. And we each have our unique gifts. The unlimited possibilities of life are available to each and every one of us. So why can I access not only communication with my son from Spirit, but also physical representation of that continued relationship?

I really do not have the answer to that question. Perhaps some things are unexplainable. I only know that the occurrences that I and others around me have witnessed since Ben's passing have been nothing short of miraculous. Sometimes I do ponder, "What is the elixir—the ingredients necessary to be present to everyday miracles and direct physical communication from Spirit?" "Does the spirit need to be a powerful, old soul who has mastered the ability to bring its essence through after passing?" "Does the receiver need to be a developed conduit and master of Spirit connection, or do they simply need a willingness to be open to what is possible?"

I feel as though my heart has been broken open. I am in my heart these days more than I am in my head. Could this be the main ingredient for the grace that has found its way into my kitchen once again? Or is it the daily practice of gratitude—and remembering to focus on the good in my life —that brings such abundance to me?

Some folks have asked me if these happenings freak me out. My answer is, "No. Absolutely not!" There is no place for fear in my heart in relation to my son, Spirit and God. Our connection is sincere, loving, open and for the highest good.

Several days ago, I was sitting at my computer journaling and checking my emails. Conscious communication with Benjamin has become less frequent over time. I am personally going through a process of letting go and accepting our seeming separateness. I know in my heart that he is still with me and trust that authentic connection will happen in alignment with divine timing. The less I try to control it, the more open I seem to be. I am moving on in my life and bringing a powerful message to those around me in order to give focus and meaning to my loss in the here and now.

I am filled with awe, gratitude and complete joy when those moments of absolute wonder present themselves to me. As I was sitting there at my computer, I heard Ben's voice in my head. He said, "Mom, write this down!" I began to type. The following message came through me as though I was a stenographer in a courtroom. There was no thought involved. I just typed. Here's what Ben had to say:

Do not fear
For I am here, I am here.
Listen for my voice through the stillness of your heart.
Come away from the noise of your surroundings.

I am always with you.
You are always with me.
I remember now,
I finally remember now.
You can remember, too!
You don't have to leave your body to remember.
I got frustrated.
I forgot who I was.
We all did.
You all do.
You can remember through me.
You can remember through Christ.
You can remember by going inside of yourself.
I didn't want to go inside.
I was mesmerized by the outside voices.
I saw no future for myself.
I was torn from the outside in.
You can be pieced together from the inside out.
Go inside and get calm.
Your world will change.
You can change it.
Change your mind.
You will change your life.
I see that now.
I am still with you.
I will always be with you.
I love you.

As you can imagine, I felt completely awestruck as these words of wisdom came through. Was it truly Benjamin's voice, or was there another force working through him? Again, I cannot know the answers to these questions, and truthfully, I do not need to! I am not attached to knowing. I am just grateful to have received such a beautiful and loving message.

Two hours later, I decided to share this message with my son Michael and his best friend Chris. They were sitting at my kitchen table making tie dye t-shirts for their band. I placed the printed message in front of them on the kitchen table. They began to read. I was standing over Michael's shoulder when suddenly, out of thin air, a single droplet of water landed—right onto the words. You could literally hear the tiny splat of the water when it hit the paper. We were at first stunned, momentarily paralyzed, and then curious. Chris began to search the Tiffany lamp on the ceiling above the table for any signs of leakage from above. There was none. As we examined the paper itself, we realized this tiny messenger apparently from the other side of the veil had landed right next to the line that stated, "You don't have to leave your body to remember." Michael was reading that very line when the water fell. Had we just received a teardrop from heaven—a tear from his brother, a message of hope for those of us left behind? The drop left a stain on the page where it fell.

Again, I have no idea how this miracle happened. As I write this essay, I am struck by several practices that perhaps together create the alchemy for these unexplainable events to be ever-present in my life: I am open, I am trusting, I am connected to God and Spirit through prayer and meditation, I practice gratitude every day, I let go of control and the need to know, I accept what is, I live in my heart more and more each day, and I believe that all things are possible. What I believe I receive. What I focus upon I create. When I change my mind, I change my life, and I choose to be the change I wish to see in the world.

These mantras or affirmations *are* my daily bread. Whether these ingredients play a definitive role in my life or not, I pray they continue to guide me through this difficult, yet deeply profound time in my life. I pray they provide continued messages, guidance and miracles from the unexplainable aspect of who we truly are: *spirit* beings having a human experience.

The very next day I came down the stairs from my healing studio and heard a voice in my head again. I asked, "Is that you, Ben? The voice said *"No, this is Metatron."* As Archangel Metatron came through me on this day, his message was as follows:

> *"It is time to follow your heart, from the center outward. You have been looking outside yourselves for your answers. The answers are not out there. The outside is a mirror reflection of that which you have projected and thereby created. This is not news to many of you. However, from our vantage point — and I speak for all the Archangels, guides and angels above — we are still seeing a huge energetic of backwardness to your process of projection from the inside out.*
>
> *It is my role to see the big picture and hold the space for a greater vision to manifest. So much of what you are creating in your world, even from those who are doing **the work** as you call it on your planet, are still looking from the outside in. We are calling to you in every moment, to seek the peace of God within yourselves. It is time to look inside in every moment before you speak, think, project, create, act or move forward in any way.*
>
> *Many of the channels in your world have brought through tremendous tools and awareness for you to continue to grow toward the light. The energies of the Crystal, Rainbow and Indigo children are being felt at the ground level now. These children are here to be the change that you all seek to see. You must hand the torch over to them and trust in what they know. They have yet to be tainted by the bigger world view.*

*There is a new color showing up in many of your meditations. The color is **magenta.** This color is the mix of heaven (crown chakra: purple) and Earth (root chakra: red). This is the bridge and the creation of heaven and earth coming together to allow for peace, love and forgiveness to reign on your planet. The more you can focus your energies, visualizations and meditations on this color, from the inside of your mind, heart, body and soul, projected up and down through your chakra systems, the more you will bridge the gap between your world and mine. Direct, instruct, and allow this beautiful color of magenta to permeate first your heart center, and then your entire being. Fill every cell of your body with this brilliance and you will be filled with the grace you seek.*

*We are coming together to create major ascension and, for us, descension. We are to meet in the middle so to speak. You see, Spirit is wanting to have the experience of being in body and yet having all the benefits of not. This is an experiment that has been working itself to fruition for millennia. We are all in this together, for let us not forget this simple truth: **we are one.***

There are many, many benefits to your world. Spirit loves the experience of creation in physical form. This project has gone awry for many, many, many lifetimes due to the need to control the physical world by ego. It is time to trust in the bigger picture and lift yourselves up beyond that of the ego mind and see all that you are meant to be. There is so much for you here. There is so much for all of us to experience in the presence of love as our central focus.

As you bridge the Christ Light (violet) of heaven and the Earth Light of the Mother (red) you will be the bridge for great change on your planet. This is the connection of Mother and Father igniting the hearts of their children to live in peace and harmony, as it has been and will always be our greatest wish for you. This transmission is essential for the survival of your planet and this ascension.

With all of my love and abiding faith in the highest vision and manifestation for all, I leave you with the blessings of Spirit. Archangel Metatron!"

As you can imagine, I was blown away! It poured through me like someone else was writing it. Clearly, this didn't come from me.

12

A LESSON IN TRUST

I was awakened, once again, by the sound of my son's voice in my head on 12-12-2009. There seems to be some kind of connection to numerology as this information comes through: 11-11 has been quite prominent and has some kind of significance in regards to the transformation I am experiencing as I move through this time in my life. I am not yet clear on how it is all connected. I do, however, know and trust that a time will come when I am able to connect the dots.

I am an extremely kinesthetic and visual person. For me the hardest part of losing Ben has not been that he is gone, because I know he is not gone. But I cannot touch, see or feel him. I can only hear him. Every night when I go to bed, I ask him to show himself to me in my dreams. Somehow I feel there will be comfort there, but he doesn't appear.

Trusting only his voice has been tough. It's not tangible. It's easy to discard, and even easier to tell myself that I am just imagining it or making up our conversations so I can feel some kind of connection. I have often heard him say "This is a lesson in trust." I can't help but wonder if our entire relationship has been about trust. As I write these words, I hear him chuckle in my right ear.

Perhaps I am entering an even deeper awareness as I continue to journey into this uncharted territory of deep listening and trusting what I cannot see in front of me. We have been raised with the belief that "seeing is believing." To rely simply on the sound of the voices in our head is considered in our world unrealistic, imaginary, unfounded and even schizophrenic.

Every time since his passing that I've trusted Ben's voice, I have been deliciously surprised with some kind of visual evidence placed right in front of me within minutes or hours of his dialogue with me. It has been months since our last encounter, and eight months since his passing. Again, his voice has been there, but nothing to back it up as proof that I am not crazy. It's as though the bar is being raised on my ability to trust what I know from a deeper place. Will this kid ever stop testing me, teaching me, guiding me, leading me to the depths of my own pain and suffering? He is still, from beyond the grave, challenging me to the core of my existence, forcing me to dig even deeper within myself.

I have often found myself asking Spirit for a master teacher to present himself to me. I am now acutely aware that he has been there all along. He, as well as, his siblings, Michael and Jenna, are the true masters of my lessons in this life. It is our children who provoke our deepest fears, test our faith, demand our attention, require us to listen, need our love, embrace our shortcomings, forgive us our trespasses, and accept us for who we are, and vice versa. There is no greater opportunity for growth and no sweeter nectar to drink through life than through the experience of raising a child.

Once again, I drag myself out of bed much earlier than my normal waking time. I am resistant, but moving. I dress myself to take a walk in the park. My morning walks are sacred to me. I am able to hear the voices that guide me with greater clarity and invoke the energy I need to start my day. I generally walk alone, but this morning Ben tells me to take my three Yorkshire terriers, Maggie, Max and Spike with me. The resistance becomes even stronger at the thought of sacrificing my serenity to my pups. The morning is my time to reflect, be present, and to talk to God, Ben, my guides and angels—*not* my dogs. They are a distraction, and I feel a slight tinge of resentment in my belly. He tells me again, "Bring the pups, Mom, and go now before it's too late."

Off I go, with my three sweet babies in tow. It is very early and the park is quiet. Not a soul is in sight. I am watching for signs of Ben, as I often do. The morning is very cold, and I pause on the footbridge to absorb the early morning sun on my face. My Yorkies tug at their leashes incessantly, ruining my peaceful exchange with the light. Ben's voice comes in again, very clearly, telling me to take the dogs off their leashes and let them go free. He assures me that they will listen to me and stay with me. He tells me I need to trust this process. My heart begins to pound at the very thought of it. "How am I going to control three dogs?" I ask. His response: "You're not. You are going to trust their love for you. They will stay with you." Hesitantly, I release them one by one from their leashes. My youngest, fastest and smartest Yorkie, Maggie, is so excited! She begins to run as fast as she can away from me. I tell her to stop and come back. Lo and behold, she listens!

We begin to walk along the path around the pond. Maggie is in the lead, Max by my side, and Spike lagging behind sniffing everything in sight. They each choose their safe distance from me and seem to claim their own space in this new experience. If they begin to veer from the path, or go too far, I call them and they miraculously come back. Until this day, I have only taken my dogs off leash in controlled environments. I have trained them over time to come to me, but to have them all free at one time without four walls to contain them is a huge walk in faith for me. After walking around the pond twice, I call them back to me, and they come without a fight. I wonder in that moment if this is what God experiences with his children. Does he unleash us into the world to express our free will with a deeper trust that we will return to the love that is always there for us?

The more I practice my own connection to Source, God, Spirit, Christ and the true essence of life, which is Love, the more I *become* that very source for those around me. My sweet Yorkies and beautiful spirit child, Benny, are a reflection of this very truth on this crisp December morning.

In this moment, I am hearing a song rise up inside me that I learned from my sister Lyndsey during our years in song circle together. It's a simple chant and it goes like this:

Listen, listen, listen to my heart song.
Listen, listen, listen to my heart song.
I will never forsake you, I will never forget you.
I will never forsake you, I will never forget you.

This song reminds me once again to go inside, connect to my heart, live from that center and trust all of my senses as they present themselves to me. The voices, visions, and sensations that I hear, see and feel are the instruments and tools that lead me back to my own heart, my own awakening; and if I authentically listen, they draw me even deeper to my true essence, which is Love. It is in the center of that love that I find true connection, true peace and God.

13

CALLING ALL PARTS

I recently returned from an eight-day respite at my sister Lyndsey's home in Phoenix, Arizona. This is the first time in my entire adult life that I have experienced a true vacation. Free from the hustle and bustle of daily life. Free from responsibility. No one to please, take care of, feed, drive or have to compromise to. If you have ever been to Arizona, you are immediately greeted with the feeling of expansiveness and an open horizon. Coupled with the exhilaration of freedom from my life, I was really able to just be me. I didn't do much. I mostly just relaxed. Lynn and I watched the fifth season of "Lost" in its entirety. I read a book that was recommended to me after Ben died, called "The Shack" and we went to see the movie, "Avatar."

Moving through the holidays was a challenge, but I survived. I am now in the ninth month following the loss of my son. The landscape of grief changes like the seasons. Mostly I am feeling good, and a sense of calm is upon me. There are several factors that play into this new season. The story of life continues to unfold and bring with it tremendous awareness, growth and new perspective.

I am now a certified hypnotherapist. I decided to become certified in this modality following several experiences with hypnosis after Ben's death that provided keys for change in my personal life. For years I struggled with the relationship with my youngest sister, Sue. I tried everything in my power to consciously shift our relationship. I have always loved her deeply, but our early years set us both up for a lifetime of comparison and not feeling good enough. In one hypnosis session I was able to not only heal my central nervous system from post-traumatic stress, but also change the early tapes in my head of my experience as a child regarding Sue.

I also healed my central nervous system in one session. This was after years of being in life-threatening, unsafe environments, and overcoming devastating, challenging events that I had no ability to control. In addition, I spent my teen years dousing myself with drugs and alcohol in order to numb myself from the deep pain of living in an empathic, sensitive, highly creative and misunderstood body. My nervous system has been shot for years. After finding my child hanging in my garage, I thought I was toast. At the slightest hint of a siren or loud noise, my body would immediately respond with an energetic, electrical surge.

Under the expert guidance of my friend, colleague and teacher, Robyn Patrick Meyer, I was gently led into a life-changing experience. I imagined myself re-entering the garage where my son's body was found. I was by myself. For this experience I took Jenna out of the equation. (She was with me and found Ben first in the actual events on the day he died.) I envisioned my Spirit guides behind me as I entered. Over the years I have developed relationships with four main guides: The Blessed Mother, Jesus, White Eagle, and Kwan Yin, the beautiful goddess of compassion. As I laid my eyes upon my son's lifeless body, I saw his spirit float gently and lovingly toward me. I said, "Hey buddy, looks like you chose to leave your body." He responded by simply saying, "Yes, I did." He proceeded to place my hands upon his spirit's wings. My guides each placed their hands on my back. I felt an instantaneous download of light and divine healing that left me feeling awestruck and breathless.

Robyn asked me if there was anything else Ben wanted to show me. He was already pulling me towards an image he had shown me on the day he died, back to the golden light of the sun, to the place he called "All That Is." He told me I was about to experience life without a body. As I stepped into this immense light, my body morphed into golden flecks of radiant light. I could feel Ben's presence, but there were no edges, no places where I ended and he began. I felt the experience in that moment of being one with All That Is. It was the most phenomenal journey that I have ever been blessed to have.

Moments later, I found myself back in the hypnotherapy chair, hearing only the sound of Robyn's voice. Next, based on our conversation of what I wanted to accomplish in my session, she began to guide me into another vision: back into my childhood—back to the core wound of this lifetime that set me up for years of feeling inferior. Even though I had been through years of conventional therapy, not-so-conventional therapy, song circle, yoga and meditation practice, and had become a healer and teacher myself, I was still unable to completely shake the underlying feeling of not being good enough. I knew the exact moment of impact that I needed to retrace. It was the night when I was three, and Sue was a baby. The family was sitting around the living room. My three oldest siblings, with guitars in hand, entered the room, ready to sing their hearts out to channel their own pre-adolescent feelings. Sue was bouncing on Daddy's knee. My brother Steve had just created a little chant that he proceeded to teach the rest of the family. He called it, "Sue Sue, the Greatest Sue Sue."

That song rang in my ears for the first half of my life and was the icing on the cake after the earlier experiences of our sisters fighting over who got to put Sue and Judy to bed every night. As you can imagine, they both wanted Sue. She was adorable, the Gerber type. I was wiry and independent. So back I went into the scene, this time in an even deeper state of hypnosis, and changed the tapes once and for all. I imagined myself taking Sue off of Daddy's knee, holding her tightly, kissing her incessantly, and dancing her around the room to connect with each family member as we circled among them *together*. It was joyful and celebratory. I felt deeply loved.

Within days of this event, my life with my sister Susan shifted completely. My body became healthy and whole. I was no longer a slave to the past. The knowing that nothing can possibly hurt more than the loss of a child, coupled with this delicious and tremendously successful healing session, gave me a confidence and fearlessness that had eluded me all my life. I wonder if these are the kinds of experiences that transformational and inspirational quotes are born from. The one that comes to mind is: "Nothing lost, nothing gained."

Through hypnosis training, I learned a lot about something called "parts therapy." Before my training, I studied Caroline Myss and her language of archetypes. Caroline is one of the world's most groundbreaking teachers, articulating the many voices and characters that live in our heads. Parts therapy, which is hypnosis for inner conflict resolution, is very much the same thing, only the language is varied. Over the course of these past months I've become acutely aware of my own individual parts: the part of me that knows I am a spirit being living in a human body; the part of me that knows I can communicate with Ben—and that he is simply out of body, but I am not; the part of me that wants him back at all costs; the part that desperately wishes I could turn back time; and even the part that doesn't want to become attached to Ben's spirit only to be abandoned or disconnected from him once again. Oh, so many parts! And remember, this is just a small aspect of all the deliriously wonderful, amazing, disturbing, churning, never-ending parts that make up the life of Judy Giovangelo.

As I mentioned earlier, I read a book on my vacation called *The Shack*. The story takes you on the journey of a father who finds himself completely disconnected from God after the devastating loss of his daughter to a serial killer. He meets with the Father, the Son and the Holy Spirit, and learns many incredible lessons along the way. One of the main messages from Spirit in this seemingly fictional book is that God helped this man remember the sole purpose of our human experience here on Earth: to be intimately connected in relationship with others.

I wonder if God's original plan was for those relationships to be loving, kind and mutual. Somewhere along the line, we as humans lost our balance, forgot who we are, and went to sleep. Part of the journey is about finding our way back to God, waking up, and remembering that Love is our true essence and our purpose for being here.

I also saw the movie *Avatar*. Not only was it visually orgasmic, it was also filled with spirituality, ritual, connection, respect for nature and loving relationship with All That Is. The main character, a young paraplegic Marine, is asked to inhabit the outer shell or body of one of the natives of the planet Avatar. He is to infiltrate their culture and get to know their native ways. Avatar is a magical, beautiful place, steeped in generosity and authenticity—and of course, the U.S. military and corporate America intend to trample upon it and rob the planet of its riches. Big surprise there!

Two days after I saw the movie, I was given an unbelievable moment of understanding: from simply being *aware* that I am a spirit being having a human experience to actually *knowing* it in the deepest core of my existence. I felt my spirit moving my body. I felt my body let go of all resistance. I heard Ben say, "All you have to do, Mom, is let go and let God, and the Holy Spirit, which *is* within you, will move you with the greatest of ease." Perhaps a true avatar is one who sees this truth—one who is able to consciously relinquish all perceived control and allow Spirit to experience itself in physical form with delight, joy and unencumbered freedom. As in the TV series "Lost," many of us get derailed along the way. I am sure this is some of the fun for the part of us that is completely neutral to our emotional challenges: our spirit. But our humanness forgets that this is just a game, a journey, an adventure and an opportunity to love and be loved by the very spirit that guides us.

I intend to come back to this truth time and time again, until finally, someday, hopefully sooner than later, I will have achieved full remembrance of who I truly am. Not only do I intend to keep this new awareness at the forefront of my life, but I intend to live my life fully, in this body, from this new place of understanding for the rest of my life.

14

TWO DAYS, THREE HEARTS

Every day on my morning walk I have been receiving a divine blessing in the form of a heart rock from Spirit, as I commune with the guidance of my son's spirit and God. These rocks represent for me a daily reminder to follow my heart and trust in the answers I find there. I have begun to be more aware of the thoughts that run through my head as I receive these gifts from Spirit, and my realizations have been even more miraculous than the actuality of finding the rocks.

This past week I reconnected with a woman who frequented my workshops for psychic and medium development over the course of the year before Benjamin died. She shared with me that on the day before his death she had been trying to reach me. She went to my Facebook page, and found herself looking at pictures of my family. To her absolute amazement, she said, "Every picture that Benjamin was in, I saw him with a beam of light glowing around him. Everyone else in the picture was shades of grey." When she heard the news of his suicide the following day, she was astounded and wished she had told me of her experience. It took her a year and four months to share this information with me, and I am so glad she did. I couldn't help but wonder: Did Benjamin's spirit know before his death that his time on earth was ending? Was his path scripted and timed to the perfect moment? Did Benjamin himself have any awareness of the process he was about to experience?

On my "God walk" the day following this blessing, I was transported into a deep emotional process. I remember asking Benjamin to bless me this day with clear guidance, and to help me to sort through the mixture of feelings I was experiencing. As I often do, I asked him for a special rock to sanctify the clarity I would surely receive. I have always known, as I have described many times before, that my son, my boy, my child, carried the spirit of a master. Throughout his childhood and youth, I witnessed him struggle to contain his *being-ness* in the shell of his small body and tortured mind. As I walked along the path that has become my daily worship routine, I began to think about him as a child. Tears began to stream down my face as my heart remembered my sweet boy's daily rituals, and his determination to be seen and heard. I remember saying out loud, "I am so sorry, Benjamin, that you had to suffer so much."

It was in that exact moment a small *black* heart rock showed up beneath my feet. As I continued along the path, my mind shifted to his day of passing. I remember thinking how grateful I am that he is finally free and how blessed I am to be in the presence each day of this master teacher who was once my child. At the moment of that thought, a beautiful *pink* heart rock appeared before me. It was much larger than the black one. I was further astounded that the two rocks represented my own childhood. Pink and black were my favorite colors growing up, and I drew them together constantly as a little girl.

My process continued the following day as I again made my way to my daily path for insight and guidance. I have been directed, as you already know, by Spirit to start a non-profit organization in Ben's name. In the short time since his passing, miracles have been my constant bedfellow. I am now a full-fledged public charity and am a little more than a month away from my first major fundraiser for Ben Speaks Louder Than Words.

The mission of Ben Speaks is saving lives—through empowerment and by supporting youth and families to access tools through the healing and expressive arts. We recently created two fundraising events for one special day: A Ben Speaks 10K Road Race to raise money and awareness of the issues of bullying and teen suicide; and a Concert to Remember to bring our community together to experience the emotions of loss through music and art, as we remember the many loved ones we have lost through tragedy.

I had asked Benjamin to gift me with a *white* heart rock. As I was walking along, I was thinking about my gratitude for my colleague and friend, Penny, who lost her mom to suicide many years ago. She had taken on the role of training others for the road race by using our local park—along the very path I was now walking. I asked Spirit to show me what to say to engage others to join us. "Be the change for the Benjamins of the world," the voice said. As though timed to perfection by the universe in that instant, a sweet white heart rock appeared on the path before me.

15

FROM ROCKS TO WINGS

Not even a year has passed since Ben died—eleven months and five days to be exact—and the path before me continues to unfold like a predestined road map. My family, friends and community are beginning to prepare for the one-year anniversary of losing our buddy. At times it still feels like a dream, and at any moment my boy is going to bounce into the room with his booming voice and huge presence and tell us this was just a big joke. Clearly, we are not alone, as there are reports daily of other children, teens and young adults choosing desperate measures to leave this planet. The stories are all varying and sometimes at seemingly opposite ends of the spectrum. However, if you look closely, there is a unifying underlying belief within each of these individual cases of not being able to measure up or not being enough.

It seems that every self-help book and talk show today speaks of the emotional "wounded-ness" of our society and how it is seeping through the cracks at every turn. For too many of our children, the world feels unrelenting, uninviting and too hard. For the challenged kids with learning disorders, mental illness, emotional sensitivity or physical limitations, life can feel nothing short of impossible. Even some of the brightest and strongest in our major universities are falling through the cracks on a day-to-day basis, buckling under the immense pressure placed on them to perform and work harder.

For me, many doors are beginning to open. I have delved into my life's work through Ben Speaks to empower our youth to be the change they want to see in the world. Something has completely shifted inside my mind and body since Ben died. It's as though the years of deep fear of rejection and my feeling of not being good enough have completely dissolved. My connection with God and Spirit and my daily communication with my spirit-child, coupled with the realization that nothing could possibly hurt me more than the loss of a child, has awakened the part of me that is willing and ready to do whatever it takes to serve and support others in preventing these tragedies for other families—and especially their children. I have always known my life's work was with children.

For many years, I have been a developing Spirit medium. Even before I was conscious of my gifts, I was communicating with Spirit. I started my early development with my sister Candace about twenty years ago in Boston. She held monthly gatherings in her home and introduced me to a Spiritualist community in a suburb of Boston. She and I also attended a mediumship development circle at our church with a gifted medium and teacher. I remember my first awakening to the recognition of my gift.

On this particular evening in our medium circle, I kept seeing in my mind a picture of a Dalmatian. The dog was wearing a fire hat and was perched next to an older man with white hair on the back of a fire truck. It was shown to me as a photograph. I was terrified to share what I was seeing. How was it possible that this was connected in any way to Spirit? I finally drummed up enough courage to begin to share my vision. As I began to describe the photograph to the circle, my inner sight shifted to seeing the dog running back and forth in front of a giant fire. He was frantic and dodging the flames. I paused, not sure what to do next. Our teacher said, "Wow, Judy, you have my grandfather. He was a fireman. That Dalmatian you are seeing was his faithful companion who was trying desperately to save my grandfather from a fire. He was unsuccessful. My grandpa died in the fire that night."

Wow, I had the gift. Holy mackerel! I nailed it! It was a deeply powerful moment of realization and, more importantly, validation that I wasn't making it all up in my head. I continue to develop as a Spirit medium and am truly thankful for this gift. Not only have I developed my own gift, but I've gone on to teach others how to develop their gifts. Today, I am simply grateful to have the confirmation that my communication with my son is authentic and real.

One week in Candace's class, our teacher took us on a guided journey to meet one of our spirit guides. I have always had a deep connection with Christ energy—not so much in the religious sense, although I was raised Episcopalian. I always resonated with the message and teachings of Jesus and have loved Him deeply all my life, and still do. In this visualization, I was guided to a huge field filled with children as far as the eye could see. There were literally millions of children in all directions. As I began to walk into the field, the children parted for several hundred feet ahead of me. I continued down the path, and before long I was standing directly in front of Christ Himself. It was a beautiful and profound moment. He did not touch me, but I did receive a message from Him. He told me that I was going to touch millions of children in my life. The vision then shape-shifted and I was suddenly flying in the sky. I was an eagle, and there was a clear and distinct sense of a wind beneath my wings that was carrying me. I was traveling all over the world and reaching children everywhere. When I came out of the meditation, Candace interpreted that my family would be the wind beneath my wings. Little did I know that my son, Benjamin, would someday be a rising phoenix. He would become the wind beneath my wings to bring a message of hope and peace to the world of children.

In the spring of 2010, I was presented with my first major opportunity to speak at a middle school in Massachusetts. The town of Needham had been afflicted with five high-school suicides in five short years. This speaking opportunity came through a friend in one of my women's communities. Her son attended the middle school in Needham, and they were studying the life of Gandhi. It was a perfect fit for the Ben Speaks message. They hired me on the spot.

Several days before I was to speak, I realized I needed to quiet my mind. I decided to take part in a guided visualization that my friend and colleague, Robin Allen, offers weekly at the Enchanted Fox Gift Shop. Robin often asks the group if there is anything in particular that anyone needs that night. I asked for divine guidance and a direct message from Spirit. She led us subconsciously deep inside Mother Earth. She had us imagine ourselves in a coal cart, moving through the earth on tracks going deeper and deeper into our experience. Suddenly, Benjamin was with me. We were on a roller coaster ride in the center of the earth together. Before I knew it, the tracks disappeared. Now, I was gliding through the inner landscape of this gracious planet on the back of my son, who had morphed into a phoenix. He looked like one of the birds in the movie *Avatar*. It was *so cool!* I felt lifted up and guided in a way that words cannot describe. I can honestly say that I *have* felt lifted up in many ways over the course of the past eleven months and know in my heart that I will continue to be. This experience, however, was especially visceral and invigorating.

Robin's voice was a dim echo in the background, but I did hear her say, "See yourself on the beach of a clear lake in the center of the Earth." The phoenix landed at the water's edge, and I jumped off his back. He folded his wings and bowed his head, as though giving me a sign of reverence. I turned to see Christ standing right next to me. Jesus gently took my hand in His, looked deep into my eyes and simply said, "You can do this." That was it! I thought, "Wow! This guy doesn't mince words." There was nothing else to say. In my mind I heard this message: *"You have a mission. You have the wind beneath your wings and the voice of Christ in your head and heart. Go forth and do your work, little one!"*

The speaking engagement at the middle school was amazing. I had no idea what to expect with kids this age. They are the toughest of the pack in the world of teens, where no semblance of maturity has kicked in yet. As each presentation unfolded, I became more and more confident, more connected to the kids and to the administration. I also felt more proud of what I was doing in every moment. My presentations were powerful, enrolling, engaging, compassionate and well-received by the children and adults alike. I talked about life challenges, choices, forgiveness, the power of thoughts, words, feelings and actions, as well as the importance of treating others the way you wish to be treated, and ended with gratitude. I received rave reviews and promises of sending me on to other schools and organizations.

I am keeping my fingers crossed. As I left the school, the principal caught my attention. She pulled me aside and told me that a child had come up to her after my talk and asked, "You had her here for me, didn't you?" The principal then went on to say she thought I needed to be in every school and that she was intending to tell her entire circle of principals about me. After that, I went to my car and cried and cried. This was the most bittersweet, polar-opposite, intensely painful and intensely satisfying experience I have ever had.

One week later, I was on my daily walk with God and Ben. I had been remembering a time when he was eight years old. We were at Nantasket Beach on the Massachusetts coast, just south of Boston. New England beaches are generally covered with rocks. Ben loved being outdoors and was happy as a clam collecting rocks all day long. I was there with my life-long friend Anne, my good friend Eileen, her two children and my three cuties. We were having a wonderful day. As the day came to an end and it was time to leave the beach, Benny had decided he needed to take home with him all the rocks that he had collected. He started frantically piling them onto a big blanket. I continued to pack up for the day and hoped and prayed that I would be able to leave the beach without a scene. Ben's brain-locks could happen anywhere and in any moment, and I could feel him locking. Trying to get Ben off the beach that day without his rocks was like Sophie having to choose between her children in the movie *Sophie's Choice*.

I literally had to rip him from those rocks. There were far too many to try to bring home. He refused to just take a few. It was all or nothing. Trying to get Mike and Jenna, all my stuff, and a crazy, screaming, completely out-of-control eight-year-old back to the car, much less in it, was next to impossible. I had to put him down a couple of times as he was thrashing himself out of my arms and became difficult to carry. He would run all the way back to the beach and start trying once again to drag the rocks off the beach. It was so, so sad.

Thankfully, my friend was able to help me with my other two children on the busy street. Eventually I restrained Benny enough to get him in the car. I headed for home as quickly as possible. He hadn't yet started trying to jump out of cars. This is simply a sample of a day in the life for us. We had moments of insanity on a daily basis, and sometimes three and four times a day. If we were lucky, we would have this sort of drama only once. As much as we all loved our Benny, it was hard!

On one particular day recently, I walked my usual walk. I began to reflect on Ben's choice to send me heart rocks in the months after his passing. I realized right then that my sweet, earthly challenged, tremendously gifted and completely misunderstood child had transcended from rocks to wings in eighteen short years. I felt happy for him, and a sense of peace came over me. I asked him for a heart rock to seal our experience in that moment, and to let me know he was with me. I was walking along a country road with the fieldstone walls that typically border New England property lines. Within moments, I saw a giant upside-down heart-shaped rock imbedded in one of the walls. I thanked Ben for the instantaneous sign and continued on my path.

A few moments later, I realized I was late for my therapy appointment. I ran as fast as I could toward home. I was yards from my house when I heard Ben say, "I know you are in a hurry, Mom, but there is a heart rock in front of the house waiting for you in the sidewalk." As I got to my home, I looked down at a large crack in the cement. Sitting inside the crack was a sweet little rock in the shape of a heart. As often as these miraculous, gem-filled moments happen to me, I am still in complete awe, reverence and amazement, and grateful for another tangible piece of evidence to prove it!

16

THE STARS HAVE ALIGNED

It's hard to believe that I am almost at the two-year mark of Ben's passing. Oh my goodness, it feels like he's been gone forever and just yesterday all at the same time. So much has happened in such a short time, in real time—and time in the heart of this grieving mother seems to be standing still . . . almost like a broken record that can't stop skipping, stuck in an endless rhythm of deep-seated pain and loss.

Recently I had the opportunity through a friend and colleague to experience a storytelling workshop. It's amazing to me that two towns over there is a community of artistry flourishing, with many venues for artistic expression. In this workshop I was given the chance to act out one of the many devastating experiences in my life. I chose the event in which I was home alone and witnessed twin tornados destroying my neighborhood. Re-enacting this moment in my life was deeply healing and so, so powerful. The facilitator was a talented storytelling performance coach, and I knew in that moment that I would someday create a one-woman show about my own life and journey. Stay tuned!

In the car ride home, I started to remember how much I had tried to find outlets for my son, Ben, to express himself. He wasn't a sports kid. Sports were intimidating to him. There were so many kids around him that were clearly talented and valued for their physical agility and strengths that he didn't even try to compete. When he was ten, he had a painful attempt at fitting in through Pop Warner Football. The majority of opportunities to shine in this small town were centered on sports. We tried to find other channels for Ben to express his huge energy through the arts, but his school offered very little in this arena. We tried sending him to programs in surrounding towns, but for Ben, the social dynamics from yet another town were just too difficult to overcome. He simply didn't fit in.

I remember well the one opportunity that my creative child had during his short life that allowed him to express himself through the arts. In his tenth grade year he was part of the backstage crew for a yearly show at his high school. Due to limiting funds and lack of interest, this was the only opportunity open to Ben and the handful of artsy kids here. Ben craved being seen, and for many years he chose negative ways to achieve that goal. The show had come to an end. The backstage crew had been planning a prank following the show—a common practice in theatre groups. Ben talked about it for days. His plan was to fly across the stage on a broomstick after the final bows.

The small audience of parents and siblings were hooting, hollering and clapping to acknowledge their young budding performers. Ben came dashing out in front of the kids receiving their accolades and everyone laughed. He stole the show in that moment, and I thought, "Oh God, he's gonna do it again." I knew him well. Sure enough, out he came, upstaging his peers for the second time. This time it wasn't funny, and you could feel the shift in the room. Ben missed the social cues and didn't get it. I knew he was going to do it a third time. Somebody get the hook. *Ugh!* My heart broke for him. He was truly clueless.

A few days after my workshop, I found myself guided to a bookstore and gift shop in a neighboring town to buy a book about angels. I have a growing connection with Robbi, the store owner, and we engaged in a wonderful conversation about our work and lives. A young girl from my meditation classes was also there with her friend. As she was making her purchase, she commented that a number of years earlier the store had been owned by her father. In that very instant I was taken back in time.

When my Benny was about twelve, he discovered and was for a short time deeply immersed in the Warhammer card games, which came complete with game figures you could paint yourself. He had found a new, artistic channel for his vivid imagination and creativity. I remember thinking, "Well, it could be worse." He had found this store where other cool kids seemed to gather, and became obsessed—as Ben often was—with going there to try to connect with a social group and try to fit in. I think you know the end result of this story: the kids and storekeeper all found him annoying. He came home in tears one day, throwing the hundreds of dollars worth of figures and paints into a box and shoving it into his closet. We rediscovered it only after his death. I still keep one of those small figures that he painted in a sacred place to remind me of his many gifts.

In that moment, though, I couldn't help but think of the opportunity the storekeeper had lost—to take this wounded bird under his arm and nurture him and help him find his direction. Perhaps I could have had a deeper conversation with the owner, explaining the social challenges Ben had faced all his life. Oh, the *shoulda, woulda, couldas!* Hindsight is 20/20. Unfortunately, our greatest learning often comes from looking back on scenes from our lives and seeing our missed opportunities. I got back in my car and wept.

So here I am, on a life mission to support kids, teens, young adults and families in finding ways to offer positive channels for expression. I see hundreds and hundreds of kids just like Ben who are creative, artistic, empathic, sensitive, intuitive and emotionally extreme falling through the cracks in our society every day. I can see their deep pain and suffering in the choices so many of them are making. They cover their emotions with drugs, alcohol, computer games, sex, excessive shopping and prescription medications. They attempt to inappropriately express their emotions through cutting, teasing, harassment and bullying. When all else fails, the final act of suicide, accidental overdose, or perhaps starving themselves to death becomes the only thing they find to free them from their internal pain.

As the stars continue to align for my life's work to unfold, I have made great strides in my tireless journey to understand the perfect storm that ensued on the day my son chose to leave his painful existence. I chose to participate one day in a training with the Samaritans—to volunteer to support families who have lost someone to suicide. That training shed great light on my inquiry and my process to understand how it could happen. I now see all the components of the perfect storm. Parents everywhere need this information to alert them before the storm hits more kids at risk.

I know that my life's work is timely and deeply important in the lives of many. Far too many children today are being diagnosed with depression and severe anxiety, and we are placing them on prescription medications as the primary way of dealing with this "mental illness." Thousands of kids are being harassed, bullied and ostracized for being different, and we continue to attempt to control this phenomenon through external means. Suicide is presently the *third* leading cause of death in our youth between the ages of seventeen and twenty-two. I now understand that there is a perfect storm that can be calmed with knowledge, awareness and tools.

Perhaps providing our children with powerful and positive channels for expressing themselves, and giving them tools to create an internal positive language are healthier and more effective antidotes. I have discovered through my own process that I am 100% responsible for my own thoughts, words, feelings, actions, reactions and choices —regardless of the challenges I face. This self-realization is validated daily through the latest scientific research; we are in fact the creators of our own experience. The life works of Dr. Bruce Lipton, Dr. Wayne Dyer, and Dr. Gregg Braden, to name a few, have provided scientific proof that our perceptions and beliefs govern our cellular response to our environment, and therefore our experience of our lives.

I have stepped into my life's work and purpose to share this vital and life-changing information with as many people as possible. I am a living, breathing example of what it means to not only survive but *thrive* through chaos, tragedy and loss using this awareness. I feel I have a responsibility to myself, my surviving children and my extended community to *be the change* I wish to see and *be* in this world, and to share my knowledge and insights with others.

As bittersweet as this journey has been for me, I hold the belief within my heart and mind that I am truly blessed and grateful for my life with all its goodness. Aha! My thoughts, words, feelings and actions become my experience. I choose the good ones!

17

THE PERFECT STORM

There is no doubt in my mind—and my life experience confirms—that there are fragments in time where the perfect storm has presented itself in each of our lives. In my spiritual explorative circles and conversations over the years, I have heard these moments referred to as "exit points." Some believe they are predetermined before we even incarnate into our current life.

I will never know in this present reality if my belief is *truth* or not, but what I have come to understand at a much deeper level is that our personal truths and beliefs do have a tremendous impact on our experience. I am now able to see the perfect storm that developed over time for Ben to commit suicide. I have certainly experienced moments in my own life where these very ingredients presented themselves in what could have been a perfectly designed ending to my own story. I imagine there are moments in almost every person's life where they reach a point of wanting to die. I have had those moments myself. I didn't have the courage to act upon them, but perhaps I never reached that point of no return.

So what are the ingredients that make up the perfect scene for our loved ones to leave us? According to suicidology, there are multiple contributing factors. For Ben, far too many of those factors were present and accounted for. I only wish I had seen them in advance. What if this knowledge that I have gained through Ben's destiny could have saved his life? What if sharing it now can save others?

That's the problem with time—once an event happens, it's too late. It *is* certainly too late for my Benny and our family, because we cannot change the past. However, it's not too late for the thousands of other families right in my own backyard who are dealing every day with this recipe for brewing disaster.

According to recent scientific research, the theory of genetic predisposition is being questioned and tested. Scientists have actually removed the genetic code from the nucleus of a cell and documented the results. The cell continues to develop the same—with or without the DNA present. There is more to this scientific evidence that I am not able to articulate here, but my basic understanding is that genetics do not play as big a role as we have previously believed. That being said, our beliefs and understandings over the years were that Ben was dealing with a genetic condition called Obsessive Compulsive Disorder and severe social phobia and anxiety. He had all the labels, handed down through time, to anchor this belief into his cells and mine. It certainly was a factor for him, and because it's what we believed, it became our experience.

Also, Ben's behaviors and patterns in his mind and body showed significant signs of cause and effect. He was hugely challenged in the area of learning, and his brain was continuously challenged by what appeared to be chemical imbalances. Our attempts to control these chemical imbalances with prescription medications teetered between successful and futile. Ben found his own solace through self-medication with the use of marijuana. He would swing from depressed to anxious to emotionally unravelling to brain-locked and back again, sometimes three and four times a day when he was younger. Medication stabilized him for the most part as he got a little older, but the challenges were still very much under the surface. He just learned to control them better.

I believe the coping tools he learned from me played a huge role in his ability to manage and shift his beliefs and experiences with his daily challenges. Although I have no real proof, I believe these were the greater problem-solvers for Ben. The only confirmation we had was in the changes we experienced as a family in the progression of our day-to-day journey with him.

The next ingredient is personality. Ben, as you already know, was bigger than life. He had a huge personality that was continuously stifled by everyone around him. He was bold, pushy, demanding, determined, creative, authentic, artistic, sensitive, intuitive and empathetic. I am certain that if his intense personality traits had been channeled in a positive direction, he could have been this generation's version of Lawrence of Arabia. Those are tough traits to stuff into a box. In the beginning, the more we tried to stuff him in to that box, the more he fought. He had a tenacity that I have never witnessed in another child. Again, we came to call his tenacity and determination "brain-lock," which became our belief and therefore our experience. I often wondered if he had been raised in a time where he could have worked in the fields or roamed free in the forest, if the feeling of being stuck or stuffed inside a box would have even been present. Would he have fought so fiercely? Had we moved to a farm and given him lots of room, would the outcome have been different? Are we doing our children a disservice by pushing them into what I view as a smaller and smaller container? Is this container born through fear of open spaces and freedom to explore life? Is the fear of a serial killer or predator around every corner at the root of our incessant need to keep our children safe and locked behind closed, controlled doors? Every scary movie produced today plays into our subconscious fears to lock our doors, take our kids off of the playgrounds and keep them engaged in controlled sports.

When we do this with kids like Ben, we are cutting off their life force.

Instead of playing sports, Ben got addicted to video games and rarely went outside. He seemed to feel safer with technology—almost as if it buffered him from reality and having to deal with his peers face-to-face. When I was a kid, the playground was the place where I learned about social injustices—but I also learned the strength and awareness to survive. Back then, if you told another kid to back off or called them a name that was hurtful, you ran the risk of being punched in the face. There was a visceral, in-the-moment experience of cause and effect. Today, our children communicate with and perform most of their social interactions through a three-by-five-inch modern-day walkie-talkie. Have you walked into a shopping mall recently and witnessed a group of kids communicating through texting—even when they are standing right in front of each other? When kids are sitting at home on their computers it's all too easy to call someone names, and this often causes a nuclear attack on one child's self-esteem. Because our technology has the ability to instantaneously bring information from one place to another, that negative information immediately reaches the targeted child, possibly overwhelming him or her, and perhaps even resulting in irreversible damage or tragedy.

Because of the work that Ben and the rest of my family stumbled through as he matured, we began to take on varying beliefs about his condition. And he began to present differently. I learned to flow with his energy—not against it. I learned ways to unplug from him when he was up against emotional blocks that triggered his intense frustration and put him into the chemical, biological response of brain-lock. When he was in that state, I learned to give him lots and lots of space to cool down his brain and body of pain. I stopped pushing him or trying to control him; it was futile to even try. Finally, over a six-year period, he was almost free of what we had called brain-lock.

Ben needed lots of space—much to the dismay and continuous resistance of his brother and sister. "It's not fair," they would say. They, too, needed their space. But the bigger voice and the more determined child won those battles in our house. It wasn't fair, but it was survival at the time. We were slowly but surely untying the knots, unraveling the limiting beliefs, changing the internal tapes, and thus changing the outer picture, day by day by day, one small step at a time.

In Ben's story, myriad past experiences helped create the recipe for the perfect storm. The most prominent event happened at the private school he attended two years before he died. We had placed him in this school after a disastrous experience in the mainstream system and our courageous— yet equally disastrous—attempt to homeschool him, or, as I referred to it, as "un-schooling" him for two years. This school had many positive attributes and helped Ben to learn a lot of social skills. It was way outside the box. I called it "Harry Potter School" to my inner circle, and spent the entire two years he was there defending this choice to the opposing forces of family and friends as to whether this system was a fit for him. It was a reprieve at the time. It also gave him lots and lots of space to find himself. He basically played four-square every day for hours and hours, climbed trees, came home dirty and bruised, and for the most part was happier than I had seen him in years. He was beginning to unravel and "un-school." The opposing team continued to point out "But he's not learning."

To this day I disagree, but wish the school had given him a bit more academic direction. Ben's sister joined him there the second year. She, too, blossomed and was happier than I had ever seen her. Ahhh, *space!* A wide berth! Was this the defining necessity that my two explorative, creative, out-of-the-box kiddos needed? It was clear to me that it was; but the combination of opposing voices, diminishing funds, long days driving them back and forth from one town to another, and Ben's ultimate desire to come back to the mainstream and *be like his brother,* won out in the end.

A few months before Ben and Jenna's departure from this school, one of their schoolmates invited them to attend his sixteenth birthday party. Many of the kids that attended school there came from wealth. This boy was a rich kid, and my kids idolized him. He used his power to control his schoolmates like little pawns in a chess game: he would offer candy to them, then snatch it away at his whim. Since the school was also very small, everyone around this boy's age was invited to his party, including Ben and Jenna and all their combined friends. They were going to be picked up at the school in a limousine and brought to a fancy restaurant with all the trimmings to celebrate the big day. My kids were beside themselves and waited expectantly for the moment to arrive.

The day of the party, Ben and his classmate had a squabble. The classmate declared that Ben was exiled from his party. I will never forget the emotional devastation I witnessed my son experience as that limousine pulled away without him. He was so hurt. That event was the clincher for his decision to come back to the public school. He didn't even want to go to school in the other town after that, and I can honestly say that I didn't blame him. He had totally lost face. It was hard enough for Ben to be at the bottom of the social pool in the mainstream school, but at least he could hide behind the rocks and blend in. In a small, private pond of fish he was clearly the bottom-feeder, and everyone knew it.

Unfortunately, we couldn't bring Ben back to our own school without bringing his sister along with him. That is a whole different story—or perhaps a different chapter in this book. Jenna's journey shifted drastically in a negative direction following that decision. But for now, the story here is Ben's.

Coming back home, Ben presented with many strikes against him. From his past experiences here he was already a social outcast. Academically, he was way behind. It was finally determined through testing that Ben had some huge learning curves. They dropped him back to the ninth grade, much to his dismay. At the same time, he continued to exhibit that bulldog determination that was, in this case, his greatest strength; it showed maturity and growth. All of these ingredients were thrown into the mix for the next three years of his life. He spent the first year sitting alone at the lunchroom table. He tried hard to fit in socially, and struggled academically, but somehow was getting through it. There were days you could cut the stress of his life with a knife.

After the painful realization that socially he was toast at his local school, Ben decided he would give the local vocational school a try. He started tenth grade there, and we were very hopeful. Socially, Ben loved it. He made a bunch of friends immediately. He did fabulously with the vocational aspect, and wanted to pursue a career in some variation of the restaurant business. He got a job at a local restaurant and was on his way. Unfortunately, the academic bar there was higher than in the mainstream school, and they provided even less support for his challenges. Within six months he decided to come back and give his local high school one more try.

This was a huge disappointment for me, because I thought vocational schools were designed for kids like Benny—kids who struggled academically, yet were kinesthetic, visual and experiential learners. I see many kids who are falling through the academic cracks today, and feel this is a huge disservice to them, in not acknowledging their learning differences in a way that serves their needs.

The sudden death of one of the most popular boys in town affected Ben deeply. During a lacrosse practice at the high school, a young athlete dropped dead from a heart attack. He and Ben had a painful relationship from the start. The rivalry between them began back in the fourth grade when Ben was in Pop Warner football. I will never forget the day that this boy and a bunch of his friends threw stones at my son on the sidelines—and their parents in the bleachers sat idly by, witnessing the attack. I remember Ben's dad jumping up to save him from this humiliation. He screamed at the parents of the boys, "Do something!" One father got up and sent the boys on their way, but we were heartbroken by the utter disrespect we had just witnessed and went home feeling hopeless.

Not long after that event, Ben quit Pop Warner football. However, this boy and his friends continued to pick on Ben until he left in the sixth grade for homeschooling. The harassment continued at town events for many years, even though Ben didn't go to school there anymore. He still lived in this town, so he was still sought out and tormented whenever the opportunity presented itself.

In spite of this history, I was completely amazed and dumbfounded at the depth of my child's compassion when this boy died. Ben fell to his knees in tears when he heard the news. He wanted to be part of the celebration of life for him and to join all the other kids in whatever ceremonies were to come. I took him to the high school football field where the community had gathered to remember him. When we got to the field, it was filled with kids. The boy's name was displayed in candlelight across the bleachers with the words, "WE MISS YOU." I watched my son walk from group to group trying to fit in. Ben just wanted be part of the community of hearts gathered to process this tremendous loss. I cannot even describe the deep pain I felt in my chest as I witnessed him being tossed aside as though he didn't even exist.

I sat silently on the bleachers with tears streaming down my face, recalling the events of 9/11 when I had come with candles to a local football field to remember those lost in that tragedy. This kid and his friends made fun of Benny for years because of it—teasing him about his mother being so *"spiritual."* Was I the only one who could see this horrible pattern of ostracism being played out in living color before me? I see now that my own beliefs and perceptions somehow played a role in this painful drama. I was also reliving my life story of being left out of the social life of my own community. The therapist I have seen since Ben's passing holds the belief that this humiliating event was a huge factor in my son's own death. Ben was still wearing his bright blue remembrance bracelet on his wrist as he lay in his own casket less than one year later.

Over the course of the months following this tragic and sudden death, Ben experienced many more life stressors. He learned that his favorite and closest aunt, my sister Candace, was diagnosed with terminal metastatic breast cancer and her days were numbered. And then our family dog Rosebud, who was twelve years old, needed to be put to sleep. We were all present for the passing of our beloved dog, with the veterinarian coming to our home to send Rosebud to heaven. We all gathered around her in the yard, with a beautiful angel blanket to wrap her in. The vet gave Rosie a shot to calm her, and then the shot that would end her life. As Rosie died and took her last breath, Benny picked her up and felt her spirit leave her. He wept and wept. Ben was the most amazing role model in my life for truly feeling pain and then releasing it. I often wonder if Ben's intense feeling, witnessing—and, on some empathic level *experiencing*—the sweet release of Rosebud's spirit played a role in his decision to end his own life. Again, I will never know the truth, but I do imagine him daydreaming about that experience. She died so peacefully and gracefully in his arms and then was finally free of the pain we had witnessed for months.

To help himself cope with all of this, Ben was still self-medicating with marijuana. He had shared many times with us and with his therapist that marijuana helped him with his OCD rituals and helped him concentrate. It had also contributed greatly to his recent popularity, because the majority of kids at his school participated in some form of alcohol or drug use. Now, he was considered *cool!* We had many conversations in our home about our concerns. He had it stuck in his OCD brain that marijuana wasn't a big deal, because it had just become legal and decriminalized in Massachusetts.

Although all of these factors and stressors were present, Ben had begun to shift socially. More and more, he became okay in his own skin. He would come home from school and say that he didn't care if he was alone at the lunchroom table. He began to adopt a new attitude. He started to make friends, especially girls. Girls started to sit with him—much to the disliking of the boys, of course. The boys still teased and ribbed him, but the girls had discovered this beauty amongst them. They began to recognize a compassionate, sensitive, loving, handsome, and funny young man coming out of the mist and into the center of their lives. He had it going on! Thanks be to God, Ben had finally found his stride!

Eventually, he mustered the courage to ask one of the girls he liked to his eleventh-grade prom. He was invited to ride with thirty-five of his peers in a giant limo for what was to be his hard-won victory of social acceptance. He was so happy and excited! It was all he could talk about. Ben finally began to feel what it was like to be part of something bigger than himself. He finally knew what it meant to be interconnected and part of his community.

The morning of April 16, 2009, all of these factors came into play to provide the perfect storm for Benjamin's demise. Ben was caught by one of his teachers with a small amount of marijuana in his car. The teacher smelled it on his clothes that morning. According to Ben, many of the adults around him used it too—teachers included, and mixed messages are a disaster when attempting to discipline an OCD brain. The authorities at school that day knew of Ben's challenges. They also considered his academic weaknesses when delivering his punishment. Because he was on an IEP (an Individualized Education Plan), and they thought that the usual punishment of ten days' suspension would damage his academic record, they decided instead to take away his prom.

I can only imagine the flashes that went off in my boy's mind when he received that pronouncement. All his deep-seated emotional triggers went off. These flashes likely included witnessing the limo pull away without him at his private school, the day-to-day challenges of dealing with the rituals that continued to plague him; the mix of drugs in his body from both prescription medications and his self-medication with marijuana; the fantasy of either being remembered by his peers with his name being splashed across the bleachers, or perhaps being completely forgotten; and the feelings of peace he would surely feel upon his final release from life—just as he had witnessed in the passing of his dog just months before.

Benjamin came home from this cruel punishment and within thirty minutes of this final blow wrote a suicide note to his family, took one of our dog's leashes and hung himself in the garage.

The warning signs for the perfect storm had all been there, but for Ben and the people who loved him, it was too late. His ship had sunk

18

MY PATH TO ENLIGHTENMENT

Every day is a new opportunity for me to practice present-moment awareness and stay tuned to the messages of Spirit in my life. As I move forward, it is through the process of reflecting upon and looking back at the stream of events and messages over the course of months that helps me connect the dots and see the path I am being guided toward.

One week after Ben took his soul flight to heaven, I met a woman who has since become one of my dearest friends. Monya lost her beautiful son, Scotty, to suicide a year before Benjamin. She, too, is a healer, teacher, and messenger of love in this world. She, too, is not only surviving but thriving beyond her loss through her faith, her lessons and her deep respect for life and love that transcends physical form. I am deeply grateful for her presence in my life. Within a few months of our connection, Monya invited me to join her Open Circles for Women and be co-leader in facilitating some of them. I am honored to be a part of these monthly women's gatherings.

For years, I was part of a song circle lovingly guided by my sister Lyndsey. The song circle disbanded when she moved to Arizona. When she left the Northeast, the core of my spiritual support went with her. Women's circles have been for me a source of profound growth and spiritual exploration. I am deeply grateful to have them back in my life, and especially to have the mutuality and support of another human being who knows and understands the depth of my pain and loss. Monya continuously brings me back to source—God, Jesus, The Blessed Mother, Earth, angels—and as Monya often says, "The One who has many names, yet remains nameless."

As I continue to connect to the many faces that represent God in this world, for me the deepest well of that source is Love. I don't have to go far to find it. It can be found in my own heart, regardless of the religious teachings that I follow. My personal interpretation, from the many religious practices I have tapped into throughout my life, is that all paths lead to the same mountain. That mountain represents the Source of all there is—including each soul—which is Love. Ben and Scotty reside there. We will all go there, regardless of what path we take. It is our birthright. It is our *home*. According to messages I have received after Ben's death, our heart is the path that will lead us to our homeland. I have realized that the more I am able to turn inward and focus my intentions on my heart's longings, the more my ego ceases its relentless clamoring. Then, I am able to move closer to the God within and outside of me.

Several months ago, I received a power-filled message at one of our circle gatherings: to come to the practice of Buddhism as my path to enlightenment. The message came through a process called "scrying." Scrying is a divination tool, used much like a crystal ball for detecting significant messages or visions. I was partnered in this particular circle with a beautiful woman named Julia. We were to intuit each other's scry mirrors based on a question. I asked the mirror to show me my spiritual path. I have always had a deep connection to Jesus, the Blessed Mother and angels. I have, however, resisted all conventional paths in relation to Jesus. The dogma has always held me at bay. Julia began to describe what she saw. She said that she could see a path filled with light and that the path was being blocked. She didn't know what the block was, but beyond it was a door, and described spiraling patterns upon the door with an abundance of light and the feeling of peace and connectedness.

I went home that night wondering what this message was trying to tell me. After Ben died, my friend Jeannette invited me to her home for monthly chants of the Lotus Sutra: *Nam-myoho-renge-kyo*. The day following our women's circle was the next monthly meeting for the local Buddhist community to come together at her house. As I sat facing the altar, with my borrowed beads and prayer book posed for the new process I'd been learning, I realized that the altar and scroll of this mystic law reflected the vision I had heard described the night before. I knew in that moment that my path had been made clear to me. I started a dedicated practice of the Lotus Sutra that afternoon, and haven't stopped since. This practice has been profound for me and has opened many doors that would have otherwise felt impossibly closed.

I am now moving through Ben's loss with a deep sense of purpose, and my life is soaring both personally and professionally. I am finally rising, like the phoenix, out of the ashes of self-hatred, self-loathing, self-abandonment, self-doubt, self-shame, and self-judgment to a higher place of self-love, self-awareness, self-reflection, self-acceptance, ownership and accountability for my own experience. I am stepping fully beyond self into service for the greater good of the whole.

One of the philosophies of my new practice is reflecting on the power and necessity of *resistance* in our lives. It is that very resistance that helps us to break through our obstacles and take flight—just like the jet airplane that courses down the runway, lifted skyward by the very resistance it meets as it picks up speed. My life has hit many bumps, turns and challenges and much resistance, but each obstacle has provided an opportunity for immense growth, and has continued to catapult me upward and onward. I am deeply grateful, especially at this time of Thanksgiving, for the continuous stream of guidance in my life. I am grateful also for this new practice that supports me in my dreams and in my determination for a better life—for myself and for all those in my ever-expanding sphere of influence. *Blessed be!*

19

THE PEACOCK

What a spectacular stream of events! I am amazed of late as I grow myself into the woman I am truly meant to be. As my new friend Marcia would say, "I am in complete and utter *awe* of the divine perfection that continues to unfold before me."

Over the last few months I have been in the process of receiving a set of transmissions called the Rites of the Munay-Ki (moon-eye-kee'), which translates as "the power of Love." These nine rites were delivered to me and many others through my dear friend Reverend Monya Tober, and have been pivotal for my growth as a spiritual being. Each one provided new learning and *upped the ante* for my spiritual development. Two in particular have had the most profound impact on my life: Rite Two: Bands of Power, and Rite Nine: Creator Rite.

Bands of Power gave me a new strength within, creating an energetic buffer between me and those who have over the years been able to attack me, push my personal space, or provoke me to question my own truth. Of course, I am fully responsible for having allowed my own truth to be compromised. This is no longer my experience, because I have worked with this rite to create *real* and lasting change in my life circumstances. As I change and strengthen my inner resolve and truth, the outer world is meeting me there more and more. It's both remarkable and wonderful!

The last one, Creator Rite, was the most impactful for me for the vision I received. As each of the nine rites was delivered, I had varying experiences and visions, and each has been profound in its own way. This time, as the teacher came to the closing by placing her forehead to mine, my inner vision shape-shifted my body into a beautiful peacock. When I returned to the circle with the others, we were given an opportunity to share our experiences. Monya retrieved her animal medicine book and read what Peacock represents. According to author Ted Andrews, the current master of animal totems and animal medicine, *the peacock is considered the earthly representation of the rising phoenix.*

Throughout this book of essays channeled through me over the past two years, I have been reminded on many occasions that we are being called at this time to master the art of reclaiming our spirits and bringing them fully into the human experience. My son Benjamin—the rising phoenix, in my interpretation—was unable for whatever reason to stay in physical form. I am sure that he was not meant to stay on Earth. Peacock, however, was a clear message to me that I am *creating* (Creator Rite) my own destiny through the mastering of my own humanness. I am learning to trust my gifts and bring them to others in the fullest expression and with all the beautiful colors of the peacock. Peacock also showed me the importance of being watchful and observant —indicated by the many eyes within this male bird's open plumage. I have always been someone who can *see* the bigger picture, and am now being guided to bring what I see more fully into my worldly experience and to share it with others.

A few nights after receiving the Creator Rite, I had a deeply revealing dream about Benjamin. I have barely seen him in dreams since his passing, but this night he appeared constantly. Throughout the night, Ben presented himself a little older, perhaps in his twenties, and was a complete and utter mess. I remember the feeling of wanting desperately to save him from the depths of despair his life was in. I woke up feeling really disturbed by these dreams.

The next morning on my "God walk" I came upon a path of newly placed rocks near the water tower in town and decided to look for a heart rock. Observing the rocks around me, I asked Benjamin to tell me what the dreams last night were about. In answer to my questioning, I immediately heard a voice in my head, which I perceived as Ben. He said, "I was showing you what my life would have been like had I lived." In that instant, I looked down and saw a rock that appeared to be a heart. When I picked it up, it was in the shape of a "thumbs up."

This revelation, combined with the vision of the peacock, helped me realize that my son's death was a rebirth for us both. For my Benny, his death was a rebirth to reclaim his own spirit as he rose from the ashes completely on purpose to fulfill his mission as Phoenix. For me, it was the opportunity to reclaim my spirit in human form, represented by Peacock.

All the years of pain and suffering are over. I am clear about my personal responsibility to stand for the Benjamins of the world and to spread my truth with love to those who are ready to listen. I intend to continue to live my life to the fullest expression of Peacock in all his or her glory, as well as trust the mindful wisdom of Phoenix as he guides me forward to *be the change* that I want to see in the world!

20

CHIPMUNK'S MESSAGE

I am now coming upon the two-year anniversary of Benjamin's passing, and another spring without my beautiful boy. Ben would have turned twenty on April tenth of this year. My heart still aches and longs to touch, feel, see my long lost boy who consumed my world and gave my life purpose.

No visions, no obvious signs, no dreams now. I try desperately to conjure his memory in my mind, but his physical presence is nearly impossible to capture except through pictures. The mother's heart within me is so afraid that I will forget him. It is a deep-seated fear that his life will become but a dim memory in not only my mind, but most certainly the minds of those whose lives he touched for such a short time here on Earth. Benjamin was undeniable, in-your-face, and all-consuming, and took up a gigantic piece of the rug in my home and life. His death has left a gaping hole in the fabric of our lives—most specifically for me, Tom, Mike and Jenna. The rest of the world has gone on, yet for his parents and siblings, life without Benjamin Joseph Giovangelo continues to be an undeniable, palpable realization that he is gone forever.

Benjamin always wanted to be invisible. His dream was to be able to move about the world like Harry Potter in his invisibility cloak. For the first year, it was almost as though he had gotten his wish. I could feel his presence, even though I couldn't see him with my eyes. I received signposts —in living color—that left me dumbstruck and in absolute awe. The signs over time continue to fade into the backdrop of my life. He now feels like a distant speck of light, like a star, far out in the universe, that has moved on to a bigger reality and has no time for this small ball of dust we call planet Earth. I am sure he has moved on to more important things and I feel abandoned and sad.

Over the course of the last several months I have asked for physical signs from him to no avail. No heart rocks, turtles or ducks on my doorstep. No quarters, four-leaf clovers or clouds shape-shifting into a phoenix rising. It is as though the phoenix has risen and flown the coop. Well, quite frankly, I would too, if I were him. I am only aware of a faint voice in my head that tells me to listen deeply, to be still, quiet, reflective. Is that voice Benjamin—or Spirit—gently reminding me to turn inward for the answers I seek? I like to think it's both.

As I continue on my morning walks, I am observant of nature around me. This particular spring day I came upon a chipmunk in the middle of the street. He appeared injured and unable to move. I took a flat rock from the side of the road hoping to scoop him out of the street for fear of seeing him crushed by the next car. My heart was pounding at the thought of hurting him more by moving him. As I drew within inches of his tiny body, he dashed away. That little bugger seemed to be playing dead. Was this perhaps a sign? If so, what did it mean?

I continued to walk around the pond at the park at a brisk pace. Suddenly a chipmunk flew across the path right in front of me! He caught my attention as I delivered a quick "Good morning!" to this sweet little creature. Suddenly, a second chipmunk ran directly into my path, nearly tripping me. Ok, I got it! Go to the Enchanted Fox and look up "chipmunk" in Ted Andrews' *Animal Speaks* book! For many years I've been studying animal medicine, so I am familiar with a handful of the messages that specific animals bring.

Animal Speaks has been a great resource. I have received profound awareness and insight from animals over the years, as I have shared many times through my writings. Chipmunk was completely new to me, and I had no idea what this little rug rat was attempting to show me. I had to laugh at the realization that this little guy had to nearly cause me to fall flat on my face in order to get my attention.

Later that afternoon I went to the Fox to find my message. The book said, "Listen to the voice of others," and "Allow more balance between work and play." As I reflected back on the conversations in my head over the past few months, deeply struggling with the clear separation of my son's cloaked essence moving away from me, I began to recall moments of clear direction.

The voice—whether my own spirit communicating higher wisdom, or the voice of Benjamin, God, angels or ascended masters—has told me to let go of my physical attachment to my son and learn to trust the voice that lives in my head. I have worked very hard to the point of completely immersing myself in a mission in order to keep my son's memory alive. I work to bring to the world all I have learned from this amazing teacher who graced me with his presence for eighteen years.

That voice continues to tell me to slow down, let go, stay in my heart, and go within for the answers. He—it, they, she and we—continues to nudge me inward to dream, envision, affirm, and trust that all will become manifest at the perfect time. I don't have to push, sell, drag, lift, attach or exhaust myself to create my life work. It is now quite clear to me that the more space I allow for imagination, celebration and play, the easier it will become to bring my life work toward me.

Chipmunk gifted me with a reminder that Benjamin is still with me, lighting my path with small remnants of his playful spirit. So appropriate!

21

BOULDERS

On May 2, 2011, just two weeks shy of my daughter's much-awaited graduation from her infamous small-town high school, I was cut off in my car picking her up after school. Notice that all the numbers of this date equal 11. Hmmm. . . . Time for change?

I have been in many fender-benders and near-misses throughout my life; this accident was a doozy. It came out of nowhere. One minute I was driving along and the next I was flying in midair, witnessing my air bags blast open and experiencing a sudden jolt of pain to my forehead as it hit the rearview mirror. I didn't have my seatbelt on (my bad) but have been wearing one ever since. This was one of the many lessons coming through this wake-up call of life or death for me. In the split second after I hit my head I remember thinking, "Oh yay, I get to go home to God and Ben! I'll be free at last of the constant ache in my heart since losing my boy."

At the same moment, my thoughts went to my surviving children, Mike and Jenna, and a bigger part of me in that instant wanted to stay in this world of boulders, obstacles, challenges, joys and moments of human bliss. My car was totaled, which ultimately led to my dream car, for which I feel extremely grateful. Aside from the bump on my head that led to an ambulance ride to make sure I hadn't suffered a concussion, I was very lucky. From the time I left my house to pick up Jenna, totaled my car, took an ambulance ride to the local hospital and made it back to my doorstep after a hot fudge sundae (compliments of my awesome son Michael), only ninety minutes had passed.

In the grand scheme of life, this was a small boulder to move, but with it came profound awareness. I have always looked at things metaphorically. Prior to my accident, I had come to a huge realization about the boulders in my life. The boulders I describe here are people who I have perceived throughout my life to be unmovable. Benjamin was diagnosed at the young age of nine with Obsessive Compulsive Disorder (OCD), and when he got his mind set on something in particular, he was completely unmovable and un-shiftable. Case in point: his decision to end his life following a deeply emotional and traumatic event. Events like that were often the catalyst for his brain-locks or boulder-like moments.

It wasn't long after his diagnosis that we began to notice OCD symptoms in my husband Tom as well. These symptoms had always been there; we just didn't have a name for them. I started to ask myself, "What is OCD about me that would continuously attract individuals into my life with the inability to shift?" Surely there was something I needed to see within myself that was being mirrored back to me.

With Ben and Tom, I spent my entire adult life trying to make them move or shift in some direction. I exhausted myself for years doing everything I could to help them see beyond *their* stuck-ness. I tried pushing them, screaming at them, begging them, blasting them with my strength of will, ignoring them, coercing them, bribing them and changing my own mind. I found that nothing would penetrate that stuck-ness or perpetuate movement in any direction. If anything, all of those failed attempts to shift them created an even deeper resistance from within them, reinforcing and strengthening their inability to budge. One of my greatest awarenesses from raising Ben and being married to Tom has been to learn the art of letting go and accepting others for who they are. The more I tried to change the people around me, the more exhausted I became, and the more resistant they became. It simply didn't work.

I learned to unplug from Benjamin when he was stuck, and to simply accept him for who he was. I *so* wanted it to be different for him, but I knew it was not for me to change it. The only true power I had was to change *myself* by disengaging from the control drama and giving Ben the space to work through his own difficulties.

After slamming my head in the car accident and going toe-to-toe with yet another unforeseen and immovable boulder (the car that cut me off), I was gifted with a revelation. In this profound awakening I came to realize that my own OCD expression was the inability to fully let go and accept the boulders in my life *as boulders*. Even after all the years of practice with Ben, I was still trying to control the outcome of a marriage that had been slowly dissolving for many years. When Ben died, I made a clear decision that I was no longer willing to sacrifice my own happiness to make everyone else around me happy.

Since then, I have found myself flipping from acceptance for what is (a marriage that doesn't serve who I am) to more futile attempts to get Tom to see the light and change his behaviors that are not serving his life or mine, in hopes of saving our marriage. It took a few weeks after this event for me to finally realize I needed to either fully accept Tom for who he is *or* to be true to *myself* and leave a marriage that, for me, was no longer working. I chose to leave.

Perhaps the process of detachment and the letting go of all outcomes are actually life practices that will ultimately lead to the final act of letting go of this earth, returning to the light of grace. If I have learned anything in my journey thus far, it is that nothing in physical form is permanent. The harder I try to hold onto my attachments, the more unhappy

I become. The abrupt hit to my left brain, which I have come to know as the conscious ego mind, literally blasted my own stuck thinking. Blessed be!

It's amazing how we attract what is familiar. Somehow, familiarity gives us a sense of comfort and security—but it also comes with a very high price. I am no longer willing to sacrifice the infinite possibilities that are available for me in this life by surrounding myself with people who are unable to shift.

My kids were never a fit for the one-size-fits-all school system that still fails to serve more and more of our youth today. School was painful for Jenna—as it was for Ben while he was alive. Jenna, by the absolute grace of God, finally graduated from high school in June of 2011. Mike was the only one of my kids who made it through public school with few emotional scars. He was more balanced than his younger sibs and had the ability to morph and change in order to fit in. Mike is not a boulder. He is more reflective of me. He plays the role of trying desperately to get the person unwilling to shift (the boulder) to move, so that he can be happy. I would describe my girlie-girl more like a blazing comet trying to blast loose the boulders around her. Jenna was, like Ben, severely bullied by the mean girls of this small community when she re-entered the public system in the eighth grade after several years of home and private schooling. The fact that she made it through to the end of the public education system was nothing short of a miracle. Not only did Jenna have to deal with the bullies in school, she also had to live with an older brother who controlled her every move from the time she was born. Then she found him hanging in our garage.

She and Michael both turned to marijuana, alcohol and possessive relationships after Ben died. Both of them went into giant "suck-holes" of their own. Of course, I tried to pull them both out! My exhausting attempts—again—only seemed to intensify their negative choices. I have danced among the practices of letting go, being a strong role model for clean living, setting my personal boundaries and praying and chanting, to falling back into the old habits of pushing, pulling, screaming, begging. You get the picture! Sound familiar?

Jenna spent this summer at a retreat center in upstate New York since her life took an even deeper tumble after graduation. We are very grateful to have discovered one of the only non-twelve-step programs that educates its guests in understanding the power of their choices—rather than teaching that addiction is a disease that leaves us powerless. This program, which works with the freedom model, is perfectly aligned with the value system she was raised on. We are very hopeful that she will come home and become a force for good. We also hope that she can make powerful choices toward a better life for herself. So far, we are very pleased with her progress and with the program itself.

The curriculum of this program begins with a metaphor called "The Allegory of the Sun." The sun represents life and shows that we are all born into a perfect and open landscape. All our needs are met with ease, and life is filled with nourishment, playfulness and love. Then, as you get older, let's say around seven years old, you begin to question life. Someone says something that hurts you, and you become angry. At the exact moment that you choose to feel anger, a small boulder appears before you. Boom! Just like that, it appears out of nowhere. You have seen this happen to others, but this is the first time it's happened to you. You don't know how the rock appeared out of nowhere, but it is clear that negative thoughts or actions created it. Sometimes the rocks are small and other times they are jagged and large as a house. Throughout life you notice that some of the people around you have a lot of these boulders in their living areas while others have very few. It is our individual work to focus on those in our own space and work to remove them, one boulder at a time.

As much as we want to save our loved ones from the confines of their own fears, it is not our responsibility. Our only responsibility is to find our *own* way out and be a role model for those around us. It has taken me fifty years to come to this realization. Slowly but surely, I am removing the boulders in my own life, finding my way back to that open landscape where life is easy and filled with light.

22

THE PEARL

It is now November, 2011, one week following our second annual concert and fundraiser for Ben Speaks, and more than two and a half years since Ben died. I find myself standing in the bathroom mirror in my first apartment in Boston, having come full circle. I am back to the very place where my life as a wife and mother began more than thirty years before. It was in this very apartment that I spent five years with Tom before marriage, only to come back five years later when my boys were little, give birth to my daughter, and begin to raise my young family so many years ago.

Oh, the memories, both good and bad, begin to flood back! I remembered being crammed into this two-bedroom apartment with three young children in one small room, and a husband who worked day and night to feed his family. Through winter after winter of continuous snowstorms, I shoveled out two properties while Tom worked. I relied on my six-year-old boy to keep an eye on his siblings while I cleared the apartments from a constant dumping of snow. All the while, I had a growing awareness that my son Ben had extraordinary challenges with which I had no idea how to deal.

As I stand there, looking into the mirror, I feel like I have just been spit out of a continuous stream of chaos, finally given passage to come through to the other side—and not a moment before I was meant to. Years of challenge and bumping up against energies have shaped me into who I am today.

The final curtain fell on my marriage after Tom was arrested a second time for drunk driving. The writing had been on the wall since Ben's passing. The devastating impact of alcoholism and addiction handed down for generations from both of our families became ultra-clear. I was truly grateful that Tom had the wherewithal to pull over to the side of the road when he realized how drunk he was. Thankfully, he didn't end up hurting anyone or creating another tragedy for someone else's family to endure. As you can imagine, the impact of this event on the lives of those around him was staggering. For me, it was an opportunity to truly look at the effects that alcohol and drug addiction have had in my life, and the many behaviors that I ultimately developed as an enabler of addicts.

I also struggled with addiction myself for many, many years. I was a user of all kinds of drugs in my teens, especially alcohol and marijuana. I also smoked cigarettes well into my thirties. Unfortunately, in our society alcohol is not only accepted but encouraged. Marijuana use has become socially no big deal in many circles. And pharmaceutical drugs seem to be the answer to just about every ailment known to man. These ideas cause me to doubt that there is anyone living in our culture who is unscathed by drug and alcohol abuse.

In February of 2011 I was honored to have my mom and sister Lynn witness as I delivered "The Power of Choice" presentation from our non-profit, Ben Speaks Louder Than Words, to three hundred tenth graders at a high school in Southeastern Massachusetts. In this presentation, I share with the kids my life journey of powerlessness as a child growing up in a chaotic and alcoholic home, along with an environment of my own learning challenges. I share with them the choices that I made in my teens—both good and bad—and the consequences that followed those choices. I also talk about the loss of my son Ben to suicide after years of dealing with mental illness and bullying. I speak of the power of the choices that I have made as I move through this tragedy, in order to be a stand for others dealing with similar challenges.

CNN and many news sources report recent statistics that 1,600 children every day in our country are afraid to go to school from fear of being bullied. They are reporting that our schools are engaged in social combat. Kids are vying for top-dog position in the schools. It is my deep belief that the core of bullying—whether one is the aggressor or the victim—is often the result of low self-worth. If we are to change this competitive "power-over, race-to-nowhere" culture of kids, we must begin to teach them to accept and respect themselves and one another from the inside out. We must help them cultivate and value their innate gifts, and then use those gifts in collaboration with others.

Right now many of our children are expressing themselves in destructive ways. To create change I feel we must first alter the language of competitiveness and comparison—the dog-eat-dog mentality—which now dominates our society. We must introduce a language that expresses collaboration and working together for the greater good of all, which is a win-win for everyone. I recently began speaking directly to this issue in my presentation, and it is well-received by students and teachers alike. It is my hope that by bringing awareness we can create a collective shift for change through this generation of children.

Less than twenty-four hours after my presentation, I received a call from my sister Lynn. I knew something was wrong by the sound of her voice and the time that she was calling. Her nephew Spencer, a sweet sensitive, loving, intuitive, and deeply gifted student at a well-known state university, had ended his life that night.

As Spencer's story began to unfold, it became clear that he was another lost boy. My heart broke into pieces for yet another family who must endure a devastating loss resulting from this toxic world. He became sucked into an environment of partying, social combat, fighting, and over-consumption of alcohol at his fraternity house. No one took seriously his threat to end his life. Of course, that very hierarchy attempted to stuff Spencer's death under the proverbial rug. How have we become a society that discards the value of a young life in the name of maintaining one's collegiate reputation and social status? Ah ha! And there it is again!

Moving through my own process of making sense of this fresh loss in my life and the effect it will have on those I care about, I am more centered on my life mission than ever before. I know in my heart I must begin in that place. As I connect to my heart, I am guided to a pearl deep within me. That pearl represents my spirit. Life will continue to unfold around me, and the challenges of being human will continue to polish that beautiful gem that I call "my Buddha nature." There are as many names for this spiritual essence as there are people. I believe it is our true purpose to discover it, cherish it, and live in accordance with our individual truth while honoring the truth within others. I will spend the rest of my life being a voice for the lost boys and girls of this world who are giving us a clear message that our current conditions are no longer serving us.

Let us all *be the change* to create a world of collaborative spirit, so that *all* children, regardless of creed, color or social standing are valued as equal, and are honored for who they are. Let's take the pressure off of these kids to live up to an ideal they simply cannot reach, and give them permission to cultivate their own inner pearls as they move through the inherent challenges of living in this world. If we can teach them to work side-by-side rather than pushing each other to the curb, to honor their feelings and to learn to have fun without the use of drugs and alcohol—perhaps then we can cultivate a world of tolerance, understanding and acceptance. We owe it to the hundreds of thousands of Bennys and Spencers who have given their lives to this cause. We owe it to our children and our future grandchildren. We owe it to ourselves and the pearl of grace that lives within each of us.

FOR BENJAMIN

My sweet baby child chose to leave this place.
He didn't see the point of being part of the human race.
He left in a fleeting moment,
No longer willing to feel the pain
Of a lifetime of suffering with
A mentally challenged brain.

No one will ever know
What it was like to be in his skin,
Dealing with a mental illness
That was destined to win.
He was deeply tortured from the moment he arrived.
I can honestly say I don't blame him for wanting to die.
His fears consumed him and snuffed out his light;
He no longer had the energy to put up a fight.

He soared out of his body
His spirit blazing bright,
Rising from the ashes—
A Phoenix taking flight.
He transcended into heaven
Shooting straight up to the sun.
No doubt in this mama's broken heart
He is finally free in the arms of The One.

His soul is on a new journey,
His presence is crystal clear.
He's now a radiant angel
Finally free of constant fear.

He is sharing all his knowledge—
He clearly speaks through me.
He's been my greatest teacher

And guided me to see.

It's time to come together
And remember who we are,
That each of us is perfect —
A divine and precious star.

We are starting a revolution
To put an end to hate and war,
To awaken the hearts within us,
To judge and hurt no more.

The bully's day is over.
The ego's time is through.
The voice of doubt and separation
Is no longer our truth.
It caused thousands of hurtful labels—
A mindset that must change
If we are to raise our consciousness
So that peace can take the reins.

It's time to come together
And remember Who we are,
That each of us is perfect —
A divine and precious star.

Though our beliefs may all be different,
In our centers we are all the same—
Loving beings of divine light,
No more room to project blame.

We have a responsibility
To ourselves and the God within
To be the change that we all seek
By no longer allowing fear to win.

We are all good, loving people
When we focus on our heart.
Each of us is perfect —
A divine and precious star.

23

SPEAKING OUT

For the past fifteen years, I have been working very hard as a yoga teacher, studio owner, healer, writer, speaker and student of life in general. I have learned many, many tools throughout my career, yet have felt extremely frustrated at many points wondering if my life work would ever provide me with the sustenance that I need to support my own life. I am finally seeing the fruits of my labor, and as hard as it's been, I am extremely grateful.

A few years back, I remember going with my son Michael and his best friend Chris to a workshop called "Secrets of the Millionaire Mind." After that workshop, Mike and I signed up for "Guerrilla Business School"—the next step in the process—where we learned what creates the blueprint for the millionaire mind. The greatest nugget I walked away with from that incredible weekend was that one billionaire who had lost his wealth and was in the process of reclaiming it talked about the importance of what he called, "staying in the soup line." He said that most people find a niche or gadget to sell, and as soon as they get bored, tired, frustrated or hit a wall, they simply get out of the soup line, find a new gadget and have to start over. He said that they spend their lives doing a four-square. I know many people like that. I can honestly say that there have been times when I have wanted to walk away from my work, give up, hang up my hat and go get a *real* job that pays the bills. I am very grateful for the advice I received that day, because it sustains me on the days that I question my own worth and value in the world.

I have come a long way in the past fifteen years, and have grown significantly in my work since losing Ben. I am now the Chief Dream Officer (CDO) of my own life and run my own healing and arts center. I spend most of my days there, in service to families like mine who struggle with their kids like Ben, providing tools through healing and workshops. My center is also the home of the Ben Speaks Resource Office, my non-profit partner. The term "CDO" comes from my dear friend Nancy Cantor's organization, the Dream Factory Community. She created it for women entrepreneurs who are willing to take on their life, work and world as they fulfill their deepest dreams and desires. It is my belief that the kids who struggle in our world are budding entrepreneurs—the out-of-the-box creators, thinkers, and inventors who naturally draw outside the lines and buck the system. I love Nancy's work. Through her support I have learned to believe in my dreams and move in the direction of them with perseverance, intention and action. It is our goal in the next few years to bring her work and my work together to create a school for kids like Ben who don't fit the mainstream model: a school of choices. I am deeply committed and excited about this next step for Ben Speaks.

Over the years through Ben Speaks I have had the honor of speaking in many schools, community centers and parent gatherings. Each time I go out to speak I learn something new.

The most significant opportunity for strengthening the Ben Speaks message came when I was invited to the heartland of the United States to speak with 1200 kids in two separate middle schools. It was a small Ohio community that had just experienced the loss of one of their high school students to suicide, and had a deep concern for many at-risk kids there.

My trip to Ohio was incredible. I felt like I was transported into a parallel universe with the same players, challenges, and energetic dynamics of my life here in Massachusetts—only *here* I was well-received as a teacher and deliverer of inspiration and guidance. The counselor who hired me was also a mother of three. She also raised two boys and a girl, and her family dynamics were exactly like mine. Her middle child's name is also Ben, and he, too, has suffered all his life with mental illness. The effects of her Ben's illness permeated my new friend's home and life. My heart was full of immense compassion, as well as the desire to support her and her family in any way that I could. We concluded, within two hours of my arrival, that Spirit had guided me to her, and vice-versa. We both felt truly blessed and are now soul sisters for life.

Over the course of the two days that I was there, I delivered the "The Power of Choice" presentation to 840 seventh and eighth grade students, then to a small gathering of community that evening at the high school which felt eerily like the high school back home, and then again the next morning to the sixth graders at the intermediate school. All three presentations went extremely well, and the kids were fully engaged. I was very grateful for that. I was still an inexperienced speaker and took a huge risk by asking the following question: "How many of you, with a showing of hands, are diagnosed with any of the following labels for mental illness and are currently being medicated for it?" I then reeled off the alphabet soup of labels: ADD, ADHD, OCD, ODD, bipolar, depression and anxiety. Astoundingly, without hesitation, *more than three quarters* of the students' hands flew into the air. The teachers standing along the sidelines of the gymnasium gasped at the showing of hands. I asked the kids to put their hands down, and then presented them with a second question: "How many of you are cutting your arms or know someone who is?" Again, hands flew into the air. This time, more than fifty percent of the students were openly admitting to hurting themselves in order to feel something—or knew someone who was. (For any administrator who is reading this, please know that I have not asked those questions again in an assembly of kids. Again, this was early in my speaking career and I was still working through the do's and don'ts of presenting to student audiences.)

This experience was a clear, gigantic, glaringly obvious red flag to me. In that moment I made a silent pledge in my mind to do everything in my power to support families in finding other resources and tools to help access—especially for the more sensitive of our youth—positive channels to express themselves. It was also through this experience that the Ben Cares Provider Network was born.

Since that Ohio trip, we have added to our presentation several tools for teaching emotional resilience. Additionally, I developed a program called The Grow You Empowerment Series that I teach at my center, and in schools and anywhere else that youth and families gather. This series is chock-full of positive and powerful practices that support a whole-child approach to wellness. I am an advocate for prescription medication being simply one of the many tools available in the toolbox for supporting mental and emotional health issues—and not being the first choice. At Ben Speaks, we are proud of our growing network and the resources we are able to offer to families seeking support.

24

THE POWER OF CHOICE

The life and loss of my son Benjamin has been life-changing for many. The ripple effect of his story over the course of the past nine years has impacted thousands of families and their children. It is my intention through the release of this book to continue to strengthen the mission and services we provide through Ben Speaks Louder Than Words, and to support the multitude of families impacted in our ever-changing world—especially the sensitive ones, like Ben, who struggle to fit in and be accepted for who they are.

Throughout my personal journey I have worked tirelessly to bring a message of hope and inspiration to our youth through the Ben Speaks Power of Choice presentation, the Power of Choice workshops and retreats, and the ever-growing Ben Cares Provider Network. It is through our network that we share many resources and education to work hand-in-hand with traditional medicine, providing a whole-child and whole-person approach to wellness, and fulfilling our mission to provide access to healing and expressive art resources for youth, families and communities.

Our signature Power of Choice presentation has been delivered to middle schools, high schools, colleges, PTOs and community centers throughout New England. Through my painful story we are reaching the hearts and minds of teens and adolescents to help them access powerful messages and distinctions for change. Students experience how to:

1. **Become Aware:** We all want to be loved and accepted for who we are.
2. **Think Above the Line:** Are you a victim or a powerful creator?
3. **Create a Collaborative Community** where we all shine.
4. **Access Your Desired Outcome:** Thoughts, words, feelings and actions become your destiny.
5. **Use the Power of Visualization and Affirmations** to direct your energy towards your goals.
6. **Find Positive Ways** to channel negative emotions.
7. **Practice Gratitude Every Day** and listen to your heart.
8. **Learn Mindfulness** to bring balance into your life.
9. **Live Through Intention** and take action toward your dreams.

The Power of Choice presentation delivers powerful, experiential exercises through kinesiology and guided imagery to affirm the power of our thoughts, words, feelings and actions. Students will set intentions with our Hands and Feet exercise to put thoughts into actions.

The Ben Speaks Pledge reflects our deepest core values and messages. This pledge has already impacted thousands of middle and high school students across the United States.

Finally, students leave the presentation with a very powerful tool: a *Mindful Medallion*—a tangible token for remembering that we can each *choose* our own path.

Ben Speaks empowers youth, families and communities by providing tools to help them develop and evolve. Through powerful messages and resources we can create a world where all people—especially our children—can access their innate gifts, choose their path and become powerful creators who fulfill their own destiny.

Together we can create a world where *we all shine!*

THE BEN SPEAKS PLEDGE

All students take this pledge at the end of our Power of Choice Presentations:

I pledge allegiance
To be myself
And to be a stand for change!
To take full responsibility
For my thoughts, words, feelings and actions;
To treat myself and all those around me
With kindness and respect;
To trust my gifts;
To put my energy into growing myself fully;
To be a voice for a world where all human beings
Are loved and accepted for who they are,
One world,
Under Grace,
Indivisible,
With dignity
And true justice for all!

IN DEEP GRATITUDE

It is the people closest to me that I must shed light upon and to whom I must give my deepest heartfelt thanks.

First and foremost, my two surviving children, Michael and Jenna: I simply would not have survived the loss of Ben and the years of pain and upheaval without knowing that your love for me was always there. I appreciate you both so much and am grateful for the incredible people you have become. Your continued support of Ben Speaks and your knowing of the importance of keeping Ben's voice alive—even though at times it has been personally challenging for you—means the world to me. You are both the most resilient, strong, courageous and authentic people I know and I am so, so, so proud of you. Keep being **you** and shine your light in this world!

To my sisters in spirit, Lyndsey and Candace: You were both my spiritual and life teachers. Without your influence in my life, I simply would not have grown into the woman I am today. You taught me the value of love and acceptance, and seeing life as a mirror. You taught me to take responsibility for my choices, and that life continues long after the body's return to the earth. Thank you for having my back and standing powerfully beside me in the early years after Ben died, and for your continued support as my angels in the outfield to this day.

To my beautiful mother for seeing, accepting and loving me through the most difficult time in my life as a mother and being a strong role model for not only surviving, but thriving in the face of trauma and loss. For being not only my mother but my friend, as we both navigated the losses of our children. I thank you especially for believing in the work of Ben Speaks and supporting it in all the ways that you did while you were still here on this earth. I miss you greatly, but know you are still with me.

To my children's father, Tom, for your willingness to allow this story to be told and for the many great years we had together raising our Bens in a difficult world.

To my best friend Annie for being willing to hold space for me to purge with a listening ear, and for always showing up when I needed you most. You are my earth angel.

To my sister Susan, brothers Mark and Steve, and my entire extended family, I thank you.

To my editor and friend Ellen Keiter, thank you. This book would not be what it is without your help and expertise.

As I look back on the past nine years since the loss of Benjamin, I realize there are far too many people to thank individually. There have literally been hundreds—perhaps thousands—of incredible, dedicated human beings who have stepped up to support Ben Speaks and our growing voice in the world for change. I hope as you read this book and were a part in any way of this journey that you know that I hold you deep in my heart.

Most importantly, I would like to thank God, Ben, the angels and all of my guides, especially Jesus and Archangel Metatron, for showing me the way back to Love and holding me in grace as I transcend my lessons in this life. It is Spirit that has sustained and uplifted me in my darkest hours. I am deeply grateful for the undeniable and extraordinary guidance that has been gifted to me on this journey, and the blessing of being able to share these profound signs and messages with the world through this book.

In love and light,
Judy Giovangelo

ABOUT THE AUTHOR

Judy Giovangelo is a master intuitive healer, coach, workshop facilitator and speaker. Offering a diverse toolbox in the healing and expressive arts, she supports her clients and audiences in releasing mental and emotional blocks that prevent them from living their most authentic lives, and helps them access tools to create the change they want. Judy is a certified Empowerment Coach, Reiki master, Experience Yoga Teacher (ERYT) and is experienced in the Emotion Code, hypnotherapy, Aroma Touch Technique with essential oils, as well as other techniques. She also offers courses in intuitive development. For more information about Judy and her programs, please visit www.judygio.com.

Judy is also the founder of the non-profit organization, Ben Speaks Louder Than Words www.benspeaks.org, born through the loss of her eighteen-year-old son Benjamin to suicide in 2009. Through her organization Judy has delivered The Power of Choice message to thousands of students at the middle and high school levels, PTOs, special needs groups, and communities impacted by the loss of their youth. She was the recipient of the 2013 Be The Change Award at the Massachusetts Women's Conference in Boston, was given the 2013 Hero Among Us Award by the Boston Celtics, and was one of 2017's winners of the Myra Kraft Award from the New England Patriots. Ben Speaks was also the 2015 recipient of one quarter of the money raised through the Yoga Reaches Out Yogathon at Gillette Stadium, side-by-side with Boston Children's Hospital, to bring tools of empowerment to youth and families.

Judy offers private healing, coaching and workshop services through her Grow You Healing and Art Center in Holliston, MA, and her private studio in West Roxbury, MA. She can be reached directly at giovangelo@comcast.net.

Judy lives in Boston and remains very close to her son Michael and daughter Jenna, immensely enjoying her work with families.

Made in the USA
Middletown, DE
31 March 2019